The Shell Book of

OFFA'S DYKE PATH

The fourth Long-distance Route in Britain to be completed by the Countryside Commission, Offa's Dyke Path is unique in its evocation of Welsh and English history. The ancient border country is introduced here through the alternatives of long-distance treks, or a series of short walks backed up by the use of a car.
The author, Frank Noble – a former W.E.A. Tutor for Herefordshire and Shropshire, now on the staff of the Open University – is one of the founders of the Offa's Dyke Association. He led walks along every stretch of the Path before its final completion, and pioneered some of the most interesting 'historic' alternative routes. From ten years of lecturing and walking along the Welsh border he is well qualified to discuss the significance of its landscape features.

The Shell Book of
OFFA'S DYKE PATH

Frank Noble

THE QUEEN ANNE PRESS LIMITED

First published 1969
Revised edition 1972

While the author is here expressing his personal views and opinions, Shell-Mex and B.P. Limited is pleased to be associated with this book.

SBN 362 00043 3

Published by Queen Anne Press Ltd.,
Paulton House, 8 Shepherdess Walk, London, N.1
Printed and bound in Great Britain by
Tonbridge Printers Ltd., Tonbridge, Kent

CONTENTS

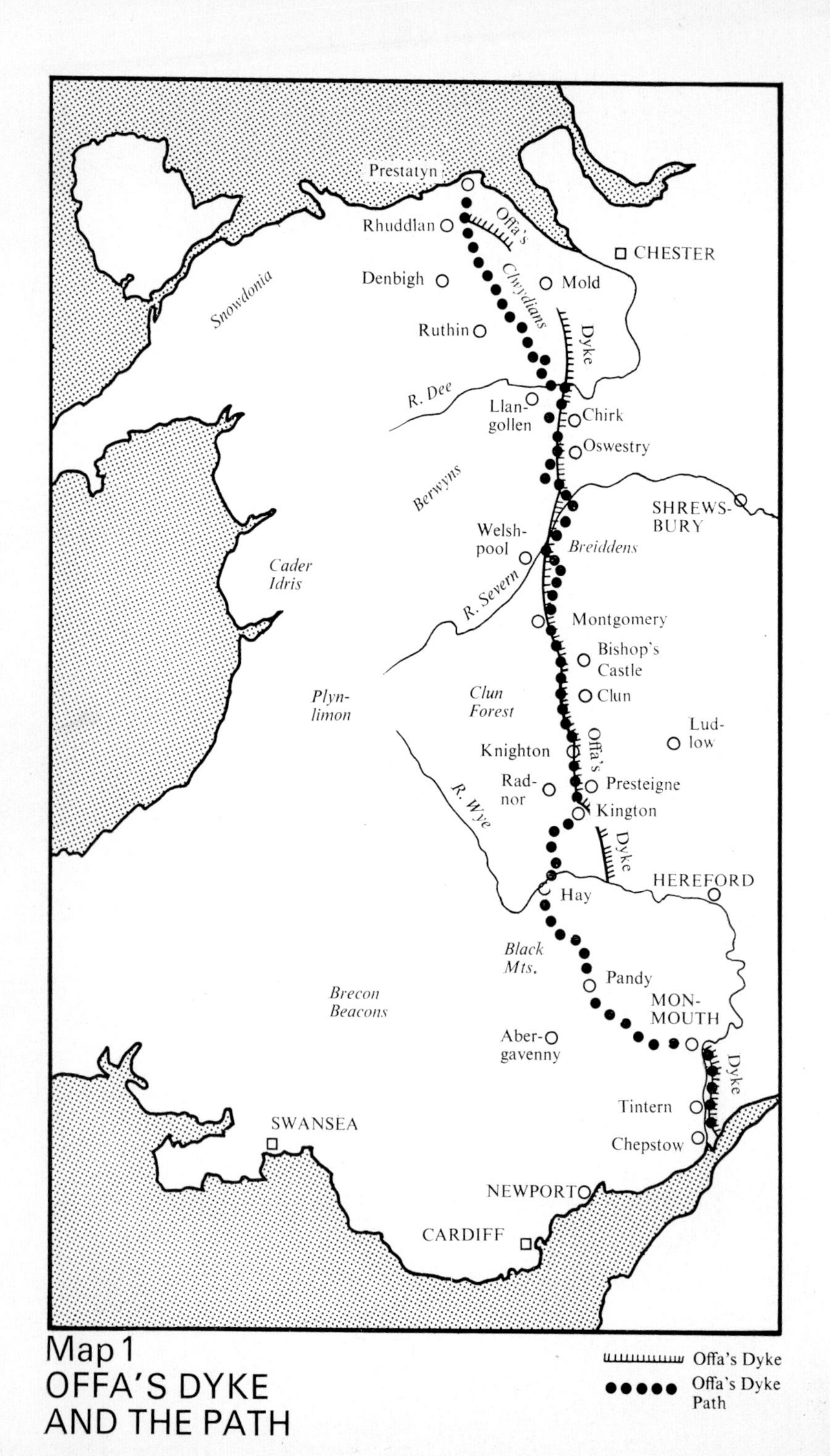

Map 1
OFFA'S DYKE
AND THE PATH

FOREWORD BY LORD HUNT

For a number of years my home was on the flanks of Panpwn-ton, a hill over which Offa's Dyke makes, in mid-course, a brief easterly swing before turning back along its main axis, to cross the River Teme and continue, through Knighton – or, to give it the old Welsh name, Tref y Clawdd 'the town on the Dyke' – on the long journey towards the Bristol Channel. Many times, standing on this ancient barrier against Welsh incursions into the Saxon marches, looking southwards to the great bulk of Radnor Forest and the steep scarp of the Black Mountains, I have had a sense of timelessness here.

True, the landscape has long since been fashioned anew by man's productive hand; but change has come slowly to this stretch of the Welsh border, and it is easy to feel a dim aware-ness of that distant past. In an age when the factor of time has assumed such a pressing importance in the lives of most of us, I find this sense of affinity with bygone days both intriguing and attractive, even if it be an illusion. The urge to escape from the noise, the bustle, the artificial values of the city is strong within many of us. It is important to provide outlets in the countryside; but on condition that this is done without prejudice to the interests of those who live there.

Among public duties which I have been privileged to perform of late, few have given me greater pleasure than to declare open the national footpath along the Dyke, which the Country-side Commission has sponsored. After the ceremony, my wife and I spent four wonderful days walking part of the path.

I welcome the revised edition of this guide, and take this opportunity to congratulate the Offa's Dyke Association for its part in ensuring that, in modern times, the Dyke will no longer be a barrier between Celts and Saxons, but a link between those who seek change from the city and those whose homes and livelihood lie along this historic border.

Lord Hunt with Lady Green Price, President of the Tref y Clawdd and H. Noel Jerman, Chairman of the Offa's Dyke Association, unveiling the plaques after the Countryside Commission's opening of the Path at Knighton on 10th July 1972

(Photo by R. K. Bright, Knighton)

INTRODUCTION

The unique interest of the 'Dyke' route is that it is not just a path, but one which follows 'the most famous of the military works of the Old English Kings' – a feature worth searching out and visiting for its own sake. Offa ruled the English Midland kingdom of Mercia and dominated the whole of Britain between 757 and 795 A.D. A contemporary (and almost an equal) of Charlemagne, he built this great earthwork when the nations of Europe were struggling into conscious existence out of the wreck of the Roman Empire.

Parts of the route are no more than 50 miles from industrial cities, but this path can be followed for weeks through unspoilt landscapes. The minor features, as well as the obvious ancient monuments along it, tell how the waves of human activities spreading up from the English plains met the sharp floods that rose from the Welsh hills, when England and Wales were first emerging as nations, and in the high Middle Ages of Norman conquerors, churches and castles.

Since then the tide of great events has ebbed from this ancient frontier, but the relics are left as tidemarks among the hills. The Dyke, the castles and the settlements merge their evidence of the formative past of north European civilisation into the most slowly changing landscapes of rural Britain, among hills crowned with the great earthworks of pre-historic hill-top towns, but with few visible traces of the power of ancient Rome.

The story that these landscapes tell is not one which can be read in a hurry. Offa's Dyke Path is no route for marathon walkers who count their enjoyment in miles per day. It deserves to be walked at a steady, reflective pace, with time to stop and look around at the ever-changing views over some of the most intricately beautiful hill-and-valley landscapes in Britain.

Offa's Dyke and the ancient frontier recur as themes in these views. Sometimes the Dyke stretches continuously ahead for miles and days towards the distant horizon. But there are also

fields, farms and forests, castles, churches and old houses, villages and market towns, and people who are pleased to pass the time of day with a stranger.

The National Footpath has not been laid out entirely along the line of Offa's ancient boundary mark, though it does follow fairly closely some sixty of the eighty miles of bank and ditch which can still be recognised. Two stretches of the Path swing away from the Dyke and the close-textured countryside of the Marches to give the opportunity for more extensive open hill walking of the kind which some ramblers regard as the true ideal. On the Black Mountains and the Clwydian Hills you can lengthen your stride and expand your lungs, leaving the stiles and hedges and the network of fields and lanes far below you. These stretches were brought in, when the National Footpath was being planned, to replace those parts of Offa's Dyke and the frontier which seemed unsuitable for a walking route, and they do help to cover a wider range of Welsh border landscapes.

It might have been more appropriate to call it the 'Welsh Marches Path', but people get so confused about the meaning (and spelling) of 'Marches' that some have come looking for a Dutch type of Dyke running through a series of marshes! Offa's Dyke itself may be the original 'Mark' or 'March', since it seems to have kept this name at Mork, near St. Briavels and at Rhos-y-meirch ('the moor of the Mark') near Knighton. The Norman lords changed the March into a wide and confusing area. They did not like the restraints of English law and claimed that they held their lands in Wales and 'on the Marches' by right of conquest. They ruled them as 'Lords Marchers' without interference from the King's Justices or his Sheriffs.

For those who prefer to stick more closely to the line of the ancient frontier and its historic features, it is possible to recommend a 'castles' variation along the eastern fringe of the Black Mountains. It may sometime be possible to recommend an 'industrial history' variation which will follow the Dyke itself through the more recent relics of the North Wales coalfield.

Deep lanes and thick hedges in the lower lying stretches will prove somewhat frustrating to those who wish to explore the general line of the route by car. The impatient motorist may

Selley Cross. The Dyke descends Cwmsanaham Hill (just above the walker's head) to Brynorgan Cottage

From Hatterrall back to Monmouth. From the southern end of the ridge the line of the Path runs through Pandy, east of Skirrid, over to the valley of the Troddi

Offa's Dyke in the Park at Knighton, and the commemoration stone overlooking the Teme valley

be even more exasperated than the marathon walker on these narrow winding lanes, sporadically sign-posted to unlikely-sounding places, which climb out of the steep valleys on to the more open, rolling summits of the border hills. Herds of slow-moving cattle and flocks of slower sheep will test his patience with the traditional countryside: until the occasion when he is confronted with their modern equivalent in the massive, lane-blocking stock lorry! But for those who are prepared to stop to consult their maps, and get out of their cars to walk short distances, the exploration of the border by car can be almost as enjoyable as following the Offa's Dyke Path on foot. Both for those who enjoy the beauty of country landscapes and those who prefer the interest of historic sites and features, the line of Offa's Dyke has rich and varied attractions.

The Creation of the National Footpath

It was in 1961 that the W.E.A. and Y.H.A. began to arrange regular walks along Offa's Dyke Path. Anyone who walked the route in the years before 1971 will find it hard to imagine that we may be nearing the day when those who regard walking as a pursuit of solitude may find the Path too crowded. 1968 was the first year in which we met other walkers along the 168 miles of path. Our fear then, as we hacked our way along over-grown tracks, was that wild nature would win and that with a few more years of neglect the enthusiasts who were interested enough to find out where the National Footpath was supposed to run, would find it physically impossible to follow it.

This showed up the weakness of the National Parks Acts under which our long-distance footpaths were planned, and under which Offa's Dyke Path had been designated in 1955. The original idea, following on the publication of Sir Cyril Fox's great archaeological survey of Offa's Dyke in the 1930's, had been for a 'historic' route, but the National Parks Commission had to rely on the help of ramblers and local authorities for suggestions of the paths to be followed and the new rights of way to be created. The 'designated' route still presented local authorities with an appalling amount of work in negotiations to confirm existing rights of way and to create new paths where these were needed; the Commission had no real power to help or intervene – that was the business of the Ministry of Housing and Local Government! To make the farce complete, the Rural Districts, who had to negotiate and confirm the rights of way, had no powers to make use of the official grants for erecting stiles and improving the paths. They had to refer that work to overburdened County Surveyors. The result, was that fewer than 12 new stiles were built in the first 12 years after designation. Everyone seemed disheartened, from the understaffed National Parks Commission, through harassed local council officials, down to ramblers trying to find the alleged path among the brambles and undergrowth. The wild vegetation was spreading unchecked over the Dyke and the paths now that the rabbits had been swept away by disease, and fewer and fewer country people were walking the existing rights of way.

After 1966 the outlook became more optimistic. A new surge of interest in our footpaths was evident, much of it from motorists who were tired of travelling long distances and seeing little but roads and cars. In 1968 the National Parks Commission became the Countryside Commission, with more effective powers and some increase in staff. Some country people and some local authorities along the route began to realise that Offa's Dyke Path could be an asset to an area which had been declining in population and wealth, and had never made much of its attractions to visitors.

At the time of the first edition the idea that 'within five years or so' there might be 'a fully recognised and acceptable walking route from coast to coast' seemed highly optimistic. Readers had to be warned that the Dyke 'must be sought for in tangled thickets of thorns, brambles and nettles', and that the route involved making a way across fences and hedges and through 'some stretches of the route which are only suitable as training grounds for jungle warfare'.

But in 1969 a remarkable transformation began, stimulated by the interest of individual Ministers and Commissioners. The local authorities promised to complete the Path for an official opening in 1971, and, in the face of scepticism from the Offa's Dyke Association, which had been set up with a long campaign in view, the negotiations were pushed ahead. Soon stiles, footbridges and signposts were erected, and in July 1971 the Path was officially declared to be open.

Official Opening of the Path, 10th July, 1971

The ceremony was held at Knighton, midway along the route, in the Offa's Dyke Riverside Park which had been created by the Tref y clawdd '1970' Society as their contribution to European Conservation Year.

Lord Hunt led the inaugural walk over Panpunton, above Weir Cottage where he was living when he was chosen as the leader of the first successful Everest expedition. He posted one of the special commemorative envelopes to the Queen in a post-box set up on the boundary between England and Wales. Then, in the afternoon he was called on by the Chairman of the Countryside Commission to announce the opening of the Path. Over 2,000 people gathered in the natural amphitheatre of 'Pinner's Hole' to listen to the speakers, who included two Government Ministers, to observe the unveiling of the commemorative plaques on the three-ton monolith which had been erected by local volunteers, Territorials and civilians, and to celebrate the occasion. The lost cause of the later 1950s had become the recognised national amenity of the 1970s.

It may not be going too far to claim some international significance for the occasion – not only in relation to the boundary between England and Wales, which runs through the Park where the ceremony was held. People from at least half-a-dozen countries had joined the pioneering walks, and some were present at the opening. At a time when Britain's entry into the Common Market was being negotiated, the largest frontier earthwork dating back to the period when the present nations of Europe had their origins, was being put to peaceful use. As a precedent for the adaption of redundant European frontiers – preserving national identities without provoking conflicts – it may have come at a remarkably apposite moment. Twelve hundred years lie behind the Dyke. There is no excuse for looking short-sightedly ahead along this Path.

It must be admitted that when the Path was declared open a few rights-of-way had still to be finally agreed, and a few local authorities had still to complete their stiles and sign-posting. Also a few signs had suffered from vandals and 'souvenir-collectors'. Small stretches are still incomplete or inadequately marked at the time of writing. But walkers have been making their way along it in ones and two's and small groups, guided by the new stiles, signs, and the Countryside Commission's acorn waymarks. The cumulative effect, within three months of the opening, was something we did not expect to see for years – an often faint, but always recognisable, beaten track along the sides of the fields, through the woods and over the hills, from stile to stile, and from coast to coast.

It is not the purpose of this book to give a yard-by-yard description of the Path. That is dealt with in the detailed maps recommended in appendix 1 (page 67). Yet, in spite of a number of alterations which were made in the final negotiations, people did manage to follow the route from the first edition.

Detailed maps are only essential now on some recommended 'variations' where more adventurous walkers can still face the minor hazards of exploration and enjoy the small triumphs of helping to pioneer routes which future walkers will be able to follow with ease. Otherwise, we ask all walkers to stick to the well-tried path. For foolhardy pioneers, breaking fences across misconceived 'routes' or ignoring the Country Code (see page 76) could blight the hopes of completing these links, by arousing apprehensions among farmers and landowners on what has been the friendliest of ancient frontiers.

It has seemed best not to make special mention of particular places which offer hospitality. Appendix 4 gives general details. The good places which could be personally recommended might find themselves overstrained. For some of the best, catering is only a sideline, and they would not wish to be beseiged at busy times in the farming year by benighted, weary and unbooked wanderers, expecting instant provision of promised comforts. Up-to-date lists provided by the organisations given in the appendix will be your best guide, and they will welcome your comments and recommendations for future lists. But the Path is there to find, and pleasant places lie along the way.

1 APPROACHING THE DYKE

There are three different ways of organising an expedition along Offa's Dyke Path. It can be given an historic character which will relate it to ancient campaigns along the border of Wales.

A Royal Progress

If you want the comforts of an established base or full shopping and entertainment facilities, or if you are a member of a party, and wish to have a wider view of the border, you may find it best to follow the approach usually made by the early kings.

It is possible to make a 'royal progress' along the frontier from the bases which the English Kings established at Hereford, Chester, Shrewsbury or Ludlow, with ease which would have aroused their incredulous envy. When they left these towns, it was to spend days or weeks sleeping in cramped quarters in Marcher castles, or in tents among the wild hills. It hardly seems fitting that you should be able to go out to the border, walk for miles along it, and return in the course of a single day. You can base yourself for up to a week in one of the old established hotels, without having to drive for more than an hour to reach the next stretch of path, and return each evening to a hot bath and your comfortable bed. The alternative of a fixed base-camp can equally allow for a kind of 'royal' progress, particularly if you find a convenient site among the Welsh hills (though you will find road links far more difficult on that side).

Offa's predecessors were the first English kings to establish bases along the border. Mercia had become important over a century before Offa's time, when Penda, his heathen ancestor, fought successfully against Wessex and the aggressive armies of

Hereford. The Old Wye bridge and the Cathedral from the new bridge

Bishop's Castle, looking up Church Street towards the Town Hall and the site of the Castle of the Bishops of Hereford

Chepstow. One of the quieter streets, looking towards the Norman church of St Mary's

Northumbria. The Northumbrian king Aethelfrith had penetrated as far as Chester to win a great victory over the North Welsh in A.D. 616. Welsh and Mercians fought as allies and in 642 Oswald of Northumbria was killed and martyred by Penda at Oswestry (*Oswald's tree*), near the line of the first frontier Dyke between Mercia and Wales.

The Mercians who built Wat's Dyke must have used the Roman roads which centred on the great legionary base at Chester, but there is nothing to suggest that they re-occupied the ruined fort. If you wish to start your journey from a town which was certainly in existence in Offa's time you must turn to the southern part of the frontier, where Hereford is known to have been important as a Cathedral centre for all the lands between the Severn and the Wye, which originally had been formed into a sub-kingdom for Penda's third son, Merewald.

Hereford seems to have been newly laid out at the beginning of Offa's century by the King of the Magonsaete, but not long afterwards the kingdom was absorbed into Mercia. Towards the end of Offa's reign, another minor king, Ethelbert of East Anglia, who came to visit Offa near Hereford, was executed on his orders, but the body was found and taken to Hereford Cathedral. A shrine was erected over it, and it is said that even the great Offa was compelled to do penance there. It is an interesting irony that you may commend yourself for your journey along Offa's Path in the Cathedral which is dedicated to St. Ethelbert.

It is possible that the Dyke was never completed across the plain of Hereford, in the same way that the work seems to have been left unfinished at the northern end where Offa is said to have died at Rhuddlan in A.D. 795. His son died in the following year and the kingdom of Mercia declined in power until it was completely crushed by Danish invaders before the end of the next century.

When Wessex had beaten back the Danes, Athelstan, grandson of Alfred the Great, held a great conference with the Welsh princes at Hereford in 927. An obscure 'Ordinance' which was issued at this time lays down laws for dealings across the border between English and Welsh. They seem to be based on Offa's Laws, which Fox and other scholars had thought were entirely lost. They illustrate our 'Border Patrol' approach.

In the wars against the Danes it had been Athelstan's warlike aunt, Aethelflaeda, who had established the second great royal base along the border at Shrewsbury, perhaps on a site first fortified by the leader of a Danish war-band with the nickname 'Scrob'.

Shrewsbury's situation made it as important a royal base, in medieval times, as Hereford and in later times its river traffic made it more prosperous. Its site meant that it was healthier, in the days before mains drainage, but you will find it a place of impossible problems for mounting modern traffic, which has shattered the proud medieval image of the town almost beyond hope of recall. Its importance as a centre of communications still keeps it as the meeting place for Welsh societies, and it is the obvious centre if you chose a 'royal progress' along the middle stretches of Dyke Path which border on the ancient Welsh kingdom of Powys.

Chester dates its importance as an old English royal base from Aethelflaeda's occupation in A.D. 907 of the ruined Roman legionary fortress. Even without Mercians Chester provides a truly royal summary of the history of the Welsh Marches. It retains the full circuit of its Walls – some still on Roman foundations – and along the main streets which Aethelflaeda's men cleared back to their Roman surface and Roman width, the unique two level shopping arrangements of 'The Rows' have grown up. This is an arrangement which is still being respected in modern re-development. Chester is a fine example of a town adapting itself to modern traffic and shopping without destroying its historic buildings and character. It offers the highest ranking hotels along the route – at appropriately royal tariffs – for your royal progress. Whether these will appreciate that your type of 'royal progress' may involve a wet and bedraggled return, such as Kings and Earls must have made from Welsh campaigns, to Chester, is another question; but there is a wide range of accommodation in the town, where they have not forgotten how to cater for riders and walkers and fishermen.

Six lesser kings, some of them presumably Welsh, rowed King Edgar on the Dee here in 972, before the second great Danish onslaught. At the beginning of those troubles someone buried a hoard of silver coins in an earthenware pot, which workmen dug up in 1950. It is in the fine Grosvenor Museum at Chester. The discovery of the same type of pottery in the earth ramparts on the west side of Hereford in 1967 gave the first break-through towards the recognition of the works of the old English kings in these towns.

Over this 'Chester ware' at Hereford were the ramparts thrown up by Harold Godwinson in 1055 when he was sent to drive back the Welsh who had burnt the town and the Cathedral. At Christmas 1063 Harold, in search of vengeance, rode most of your border way from Hereford to Rhuddlan to try to surprise Gruffydd, the Welsh prince there. Gruffydd escaped, only to be hounded remorselessly to death the following year. His widow, Ealdyth the Fair, grand-daughter of Lady Godiva, became Harold's Queen, and was widowed again, before another year was out, when Harold was killed at the battle of Hastings.

A Baronial Expedition or Knight's Tour

If a royal progress seems too luxurious or too unadventurous, you may prefer to follow in the wake of the Norman Barons, who built their castles on the Marches of Wales. Almost all the market towns which lie close to the line of the Path grew up around one of these baronial castles. Many can still offer accommodation of a 'lordly' standard, where it is possible to stay for a couple of nights while you investigate the adjacent stretch of frontier. In future they may also be able to offer convenient camping and caravan sites, but at present there are few of these along the border. Finding a new site every day along the switchback roads may make a caravanning version of a 'Knights Tour' altogether too uncertain and complicated. But for those who do prefer to move on every day to another place, there is an adequate chain of hotels and inns within four or five miles of the line of the Path. Many of these are in villages which show the remains of the small castle of a Norman knight who held land under one of the Marcher Barons.

In Norman times three great Earls were first established at Hereford, Chester and Shrewsbury, but these powerful earldoms soon appeared to menace the Crown. Hereford was suppressed as early as 1075, Shrewsbury in 1102 and only Chester retained its semi-independent Earls into the thirteenth century. Their followers were left holding their castles in the border territories and the conquered Welsh lands, as Lords Marchers.

The advance bases established by the Earls have not all survived to offer 'baronial' facilities for modern travellers. Chepstow and Monmouth, founded by William fitz Osbern, the Conqueror's most powerful follower, certainly do, but his other bases at Ewyas Harold and Clifford have not thrived. Montgomery, given the name of the first Earl of Shrewsbury, Roger de Montgomery, is a sleepy little place, but Oswestry, the castle-town of their sheriffs, has lost some of its historic character in the growth which has provided adequate modern facilities there. Rhuddlan, the advance base of the Earls of Chester, at times a palace of the Welsh princes, is perhaps the most disappointing as a centre in spite of the well-kept ruins of the castle which Edward I built when he proposed to make this a royal cathedral city.

To fill the gaps, or find alternatives, you can follow the second wave of Marcher Lords, from the time of William Rufus onwards. As an alternative to Chepstow or Monmouth you can find accommodation near the ruins of Tintern Abbey.

Further north, you could advance into Wales to Abergavenny, on a Roman site, but perhaps too busy with modern affairs; a contrast with Radnor where Abergavenny's most notorious de Braos lords had their earliest frontier castle. Even on Welsh border reckoning, which accepts places of a thousand people as towns, Radnor has only been a village since the County Courts moved to Presteigne three centuries ago. Presteigne has some advantages as a present-day base, though it has only twelve hundred inhabitants. The Mortimers of Wigmore never maintained an important castle there and it grew up round the fine church, one of the few along the border which can show Saxon features.

By contrast Hay-on-Wye is a remarkably compact little fortress town which may have been built in the 1150s by Roger, Earl of Hereford, to try to block the 'royal progress' of Henry II (whose 'Fair Rosamund' lived in the neighbouring castle at Clifford). But Roger had second thoughts about rebellion and left his ally, Mortimer or Wigmore, to stand the King's onslaught.

The Pillar of Eliseg: the outstanding monument of the Dark Ages on the border, at Valle Crucis above Llangollen

The Monnow Bridge at Monmouth, an almost unique survival in Britain, guards the route out of this pleasant old town

Offa's Dyke on Clun Forest. The finest stretches are found where the earthwork crosses these rolling uplands, but the ancient frontier provides the theme of the whole path

raiders), for two or three days along the path. Increasing numbers of houses and farms along the route are offering bed and breakfast, and others who have not considered it will find you a meal and somewhere to sleep – especially if you are carrying your own sleeping bag. If you can set out without a rigid schedule and take things as they come, then you allow for those happy strokes of fortune which seem part of the character of the Marches – just as the grey sheets of cloud over Wales, or the Midland murks, break unexpectedly into 'sunny intervals' along the border hills. There are too many stiles to climb for easy carrying of lightweight camping gear. If you trust to providence you must be prepared to accept bad luck philosophically. Less carefree walkers should telephone ahead in the morning. Organised catering for walkers along Offa's Dyke Path will always lag behind the fine weather demand, and those who wander unbooked must be prepared to sleep in unlikely places.

We hear less in history about the ordinary people of the border than about kings, princes and barons, but the 'Ordinance for the Dunsaete' mentioned earlier as a version of Offa's frontier regulations, probably re-issued by Athelstan, may help us to understand the purpose of the Dyke. The laws are particularly concerned about the procedure for tracking and recovering cattle which had been rustled across the border (this was the 'Wild West' for over a thousand years). They also laid down that neither English nor Welsh were to cross the border without an appointed guide from the other side, who was to make sure that they returned safely and committed no offences. It was laid down that only half the usual death-fine need be paid for either an Englishman or a Welshman who was killed on the wrong side of the border, but there is no mention of the supposed law that any Welshman found carrying weapons on the English side of the Dyke should have his right hand cut off. These laws are remarkably fair and civilised for their period. They include the first mention of a jury in English law, six English and six Welsh, who would explain the laws to their people.

In Norman times the semi-independent lordships and bitter struggles with the Welsh, meant that there was less protection for ordinary people. Up to the end of the Middle Ages the Welsh Marches remained a notorious hiding-place for outlaws.

Under the Tudors the old border lawlessness subsided. Wales seemed remarkably reconciled to the Union, and there was no attempt to find nationalist advantage in the Civil War between Charles I and Parliament, when the dilapidated border castles were patched up for their last military struggles. Chester, Shrewsbury, Ludlow and Hereford once more acted as royal military bases. In the last desperate struggles of 1645 armies led by the King of England marched again along the border lanes, trying to relieve his garrisons besieged in Hereford and Chester. It was from the walls of Chester that the King saw his last army defeated at Rowton Heath.

Since the Civil Wars this border has been one of the most peaceful parts of the world, so peaceful that it has become almost a forgotten land. It is hoped that this brief guide will help you to find your way, and provide a key to one of the most interesting areas of the British Isles.

Transport

The 'royal progress' and the 'baronial expedition' do face you with a specific difficulty; in order to walk a reasonable distance along the Path in the course of a day, you need someone who can drive the car from the starting point and meet you at the end of the day. It is seldom possible, except perhaps in the Lower Wye and Clwydian stretches of the route, to complete a return 'leg' of a day's journey by public transport. The surviving skeleton of the railway system still provides links for walks of two or three days between Chepstow, Abergavenny, Knighton, Welshpool, Chirk or Ruabon and Prestatyn. If you have plenty of time some very pleasant days can be spent walking circuit routes back to a car at a strategic point, but this will more than double the distance before you have covered the whole of the Offa's Dyke Path.

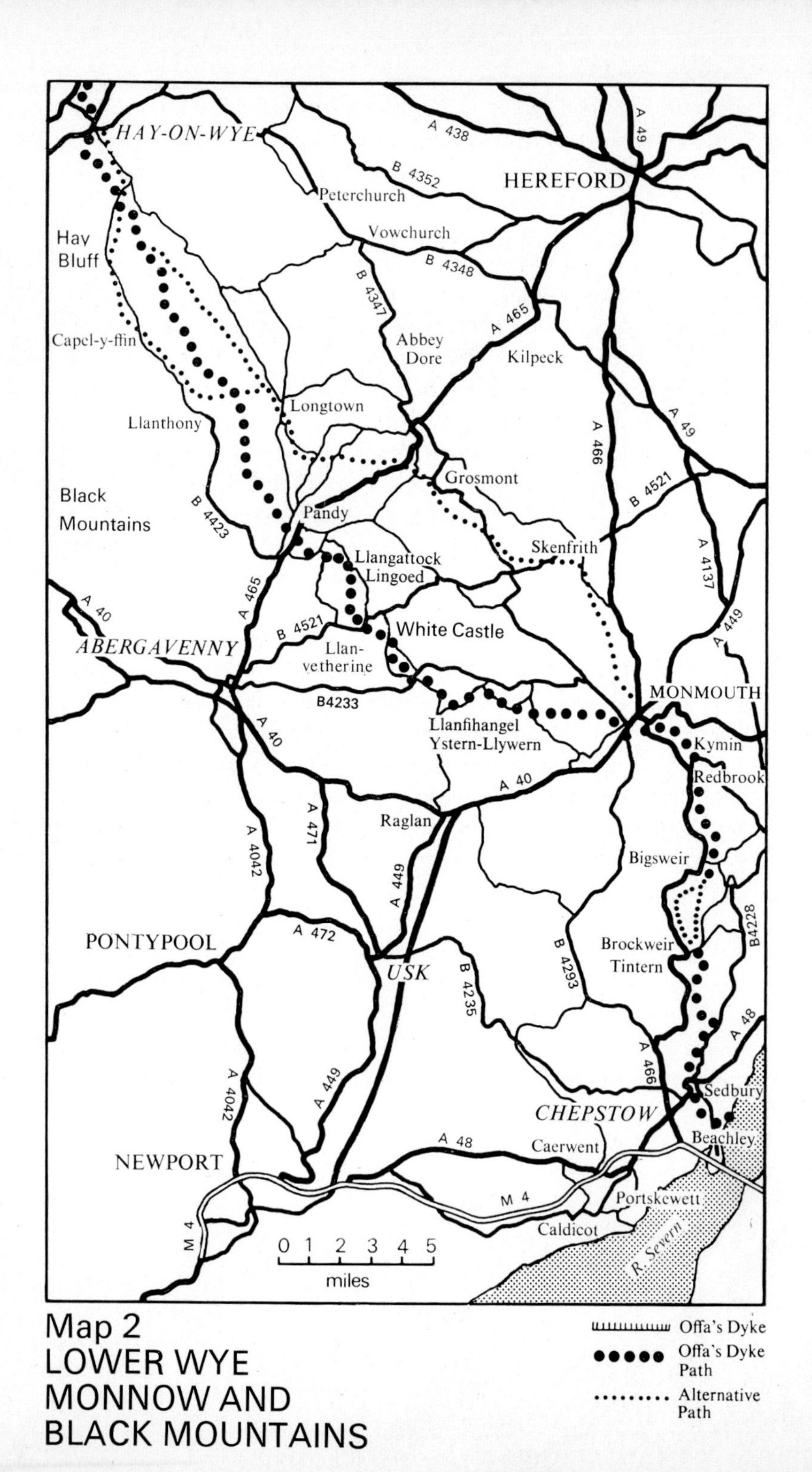

Map 2
LOWER WYE
MONNOW AND
BLACK MOUNTAINS

2 THE LOWER WYE AND MONNOW VALLEYS

It is possible to cover the entire southern sector of the Path from a 'royal' base at Hereford, but, like the first Norman earl of the region, you will probably prefer to establish an advance post for the lower Wye in the vicinity of Chepstow.

To find the beginning of Offa's Dyke and the Long-distance Path, take the Beachley bus, which leaves every half-hour from Chepstow's main street, or drive out on the A48. Cross the narrow cast-iron bridge designed by Rennie in 1816 and climb the long bend, with superb views back to Chepstow Castle and the Wye, then turn right on the Beachley road (B4228). You leave your vehicle on reaching the point where the Beachley peninsula comes into view, as the road tops the rise at Buttington Tump, on the line of Offa's Dyke. From here you will see the great span of the Severn Bridge stretching gracefully over to Aust cliff, across the treacherous waters where Wye and Severn meet in the ebb and flow of some of the most powerful tides in the world.

Between Buttington Tump and Sedbury Cliff lies a fine stretch of Offa's Dyke, though it has been sadly neglected, and rights of access from the Sedbury Park drive have been uncertain. You cross railings on the right and follow the bank along the edge of the field until you reach a much larger, and more overgrown, bank and ditch. This dips into a marshy hollow, which you must skirt on the left before moving on up through the gorse to the boulder that tops the cliff.

Fox found this point extraordinarily impressive, with its wide views over land and sea to south and west summing up eighty miles of Dyke and one dominant idea – the visual control of enemy country. He concluded that, 'On this now silent and deserted spot at the south-western limit of his Mercian

Chepstow Castle from the Wye bridge. First established by the Conqueror's companion, William FitzOsbern, Earl of Hereford, it towers above one of the few crossing places in the Lower Wye gorge

Tintern Abbey can be glimpsed from the Offa's Dyke Path through the steep woodlands, a view described in one of Wordsworth's poems

Brockweir village. Offa's Dyke cuts across the side valley from the woods beyond, and the alternative path along the riverside comes down through the village

The Naval Temple on the Kymin erected to commemorate British naval victories in the 18th century wars

Bigsweir Bridge. The Path runs on the other bank of the Wye. On the skyline stand St Briavel's Church and Castle

end of the Roman period the tribal name had been forgotten, and the people of this part of Monmouthshire came into history as the 'Men of (G)went'.

Mathern – south of the A48, beyond the motorway – has a fine mediaeval church, and the remains of a palace of the Bishop of Llandaff, on a site of the early Christian kings of Gwent. Between Portskewett and Caerwent, you can inspect the important castle remains at Caldicot, and compare them with the remarkably fine sequence of halls and towers in Chepstow Castle.

It is possible to cover all these sites on foot from Chepstow, as a day's introduction to walking and history. But the footpaths are neglected, and the area is bitten into by new roads, wire-scapes and modern building development. It will be necessary to plot your route with care.

William fitz Osbern's great Hall-Keep in Chepstow, built with stones and tiles from the ruins of Caerwent, is a remarkable survival, two-thirds the size of the Conqueror's own Tower of London, and impregnably sited on sheer limestone cliffs overlooking the Wye. The round towers added by the Marshalls (Earls of Pembroke) between 1189 and 1245, and the great tower and halls added by Roger Bigod (earl of Norfolk) between 1270 and 1300, illustrate the development of the stone castle in Britain – with human sidelights such as the great 'garderobe', jettied out a hundred feet above the river.

Chepstow itself, with its church, street pattern, walls and surviving fortified gateway (an incredible survival across what was the main route into South Wales!), shows how such mediaeval towns grew up alongside military strongholds, and developed through the centuries into busy little commercial centres. Here you can obtain most of your requirements for your journey, and select from a wide range of accommodation.

Offa may have set his Dyke to control traffic, but there is no recognisable section of it either at the point where the Roman road crossed the Wye, north of Chepstow Castle, or at the later crossing-point, by the present bridge, to the Welsh shipmen's settlement of Striguil (*Ystraigl* – 'the bend'). Although the use of the English name *Cheap Stow* (market place) did not become general until the later Middle Ages, the name, taken with the apparent absence of the Dyke at this crucial point, has led some people to argue that Offa must have established a bridge-head settlement on the Welsh side of the river.

It is on the English side that the Path turns left over a stile off the lane which links the A48 and the B4228. It leads up by the ruins of Twtshill Tower – probably a 16th century coast-guard beacon. Traces of Offa's Dyke along this stretch are scarcely recognisable from the Path, which follows a complicated course between its line and that of the B4228 road until they come together where Wintour's Leap plunges sheer from the roadside.

It is impossible to imagine how the Civil War escape of Sir John Wintour from pursuing Parliamentary soldiers, by riding over a steep cliff on Beachley, could have come to be linked with this 200ft. precipice, where no horse or rider could have survived such a leap.

Remains of Iron Age fortifications across the neck of the Lancaut peninsular seem to have been adopted as part of the Dyke, but the Path follows the road, cuts through the wood to the right, then along the road again, until, a mile beyond Wintour's Leap, past Dennell Hill House, you will find a stile on the left, opposite a cottage. Here you may follow the path to rediscover the Dyke as a modest, overgrown bank running north along the upper edge of steep wooded slopes, round the head of 'the Slade'.

The path now follows the Dyke down steeply to cross first the quarry road, then the forestry track (these join higher up to provide a convenient access to the B4228) on the other side of the hollow. From here, you can follow Offa's work through two more miles of tangled, badger-haunted woodland, looking out for the zig-zag which leads to the magnificent viewpoint on Shorn Cliff.

From here you may walk on with mounting amazement as the great earth bank becomes larger and larger, while glimpses through the trees reveal the vast scale of the great gorge of the river below. At the Devil's Pulpit, a second rock outcrop commanding a view down to Tintern Abbey, six hundred feet below, you can pause and try to puzzle out the purpose of Offa's work – built on such a massive scale at a point where the natural strength of the frontier formed by the dangerous tidal river is most apparent.

It hardly seems realistic of Fox to have argued that this was a concession to Welsh shipmen trading up the Wye, thereby giving them the use of both banks of the river. The Dyke in these stretches is most massively built at precisely the point where it made a dramatic feature in the landscape. A point, moreover, immediately opposite Tintern – at that time the possession of the King of Gwent, and only subsequently granted by their successors, the Norman lords of Chepstow, to the Cistercian monks. There was an element of personal display in this; an emulation of the saga hero, on whom Offa moulded his life.

There are ways down to Tintern, commanding the views celebrated in Wordsworth's *Lines,* but the Path follows the massive Dyke, now proposed for proper conservation as an Ancient Monument, until it turns down towards the Brockweir valley and emerges from the woods as a much diminished feature. Alternative routes, one tracing fragments of the Dyke along the tangled lanes of St. Briavel's Common, then down the steep woods to join the gentler route, which has passed down through Brockweir and along the riverside, where they meet by Bigsweir bridge, provide an energetic or a leisurely way.

From here, if so inclined, you can return by car or 'bus to Chepstow. Alternatively, you can turn up the hill to the village of St. Briavels in readiness for the next stage of the journey. A Youth Hostel occupies the Castle, with its fine Edwardian Gatehouse, from which the King's constables administered the royal Forest of Dean, but the village is otherwise aloof from the tourist bustle of the valley.

You will find the Dyke again half a mile up the road which forks off the A466, east of Bigsweir – alongside a narrow, surfaced lane running north by Wyegate Woods, where forestry bulldozers have been at work. The Path leaves the lane and crosses the Dyke, where this begins to climb more steeply, and follows this lower route through woods which are being cut down for extensive re-planting. Above the path rise the boulder-strewn slopes where the Dyke turns directly upwards to meet the crest of the slope. Two hundred yards further on, the path and the diagonally descending Dyke rejoin and follow the upper edge of the woodland across field stiles to Coxbury.

Beyond this isolated farm, the Dyke turns up across the overgrown lane and into the woods along the edge of Highbury Plain. Fox found this area impenetrable forty years ago; it had been abandoned as farming land fifty years before that, and had reverted to scrub woodland. Now the saplings have grown high enough to shade out the undergrowth, and it is no more difficult than many other woodland stretches. This casts some doubt on Fox's explanation that no Dyke was built thirty miles north of Highbury because of inpenetrable 'primeval damp oakwood' on the marls of Herefordshire. Old oakwood is seldom impenetrable on foot.

After twelve miles along the Dyke, you will miss it as you descend to Redbrook, a small, formerly industrial, village which caters for visitors on a modest scale. From the main road the designated Path bears up to the right, along the B4231 for a quarter of a mile. It then forks up to the left, and follows the farm lane and the paths beyond, along the crest of the hill to the 'Naval Temple' on the Kymin. Nelson, Emma and Sir William visited this memorial to 18th century British admirals and their victories, on Nelson's tour in 1802.

From here, the Path descends steeply to the A4136 into Monmouth. As an alternative route from Redbrook, it is possible to follow the shorter path along the bank of the River Wye.

Crossing the Wye bridge and the new trunk road, you have only to turn left and then right to reach the local History Museum, under the Nelson Museum. Here the story of Monmouth is fascinatingly displayed. Beyond the Museum lies Agincourt Square, the centre of the town. The ruins of the Castle, and the mansion built by the Duke of Beaufort on the site where Henry V was born, can be seen from the lane opposite the Shirehall – but they look more impressive from the other side of the Monnow. The wide Monnow Street (with the 'bus station opposite the main car-park) leads to the fortified Gatehouse on the Monnow Bridge, which is the most attractive survival of Monmouth's vivid history.

Monmouth is another good base for the southern end of the Path – an obvious centre of communications from Roman times.

Llanfihangel Ystern Llewern. The Path passes below the isolated church, said to have been founded on the spot where Ynyr, King of Gwent, escaped onto dry land from a bog into which he had stumbled

Llangattock Lingoed. The Path comes through the churchyard in the isolated village, with a single inn and shop; one of the quiet places along the Path

Grosmont Castle. The 13th century castle was once used as a hunting lodge by the Dukes of Lancaster

Llanthony An inn nestles in the ruins of the Augustinian Priory in the narrow Honddu valley, established by the de Lacies in 1108 and rebuilt at the end of the 12th century

Skirrid from the Path above Pandy. The route crosses the valley from the left of the skyline

Ponies and Pen-y-beacon. The Black Mountains have become favourite territory for pony-trekking. Ponies have become as numerous as sheep on their grassy flanks

Hatterall Ridge. The long flat-topped ridge is the most extensive stretch of open hill-walking, but one which can be dangerous in mist or cloud

But Monmouth Borough have been very slow in completing and waymarking the stretches of Path in their area. The route is difficult enough through the housing estates west of the Monnow bridge. It has been almost impossible past the derelict Bailey Pits farms, or alongside the deep ravine which appears on maps as though it were a country lane to the almost vanished site of Old Bailey Pits.

From the county area boundary in the woods beyond, however, a vast amount of waymarking and stile and footbridge construction has marked out the route. It joins the road from Wonastow near Lower Hendre. The Path turns off towards the Troddi, but continues on the east side, past the site of a vanished Cistercian Abbey of Grace-Dieu before it crosses the river at the next road bridge. Beyond this the Path turns back across the fields to the southern bank, and follows it to the farm track past Sunnybank. From the north side of Llanfihangel-ystern-llewern it runs south-westwards to the metalled lane, which it leaves within half a mile to cut along the fields past the Grange and across to Penrhos farm. The lane crosses the Troddi again near the remarkable church of Llantilio Croesenny.

From Hostry Inn field paths lead to Tredam and lanes to White Castle one of the most impressive of the border strongholds. This was the garrison outpost of the "Three Castles" Lordship of Hubert de Burgh and Edmund of Lancaster. All three castles are impressively maintained by the Ministry of Works, and admission to the other two – Skenfrith and Grosmont, on the suggested alternative route – is free.

From White Castle Farm the Path descends to cross the Troddi again to Caggle Street, then turns left up the lane on the other side of the B4521, then right, up the deep holloway and right again along the overgrown track which joins the farm way to Little Pool Hall. Across the fields and along the lane past Old Court, the Path turns off, opposite the next farm, to climb the field to Llangattock Lingoed church. Up past the door of the old School and round the back a series of new stiles at footbridges run northwest to the metalled lane, but soon leave this to go along the field side left of Llanerch Farm and on to the Campstone Hill road. Just west of the road junction the Path strikes diagonally north along the side of the hill towards a long-disputed access to the main road at Glannant, south of Pandy.

An alternative route, ending a few miles to the north, has been worked out from Monmouth. This traverses the high ground east of the Monnow, past Pembridge Castle, and turns down to cross the river by Skenfrith Castle. The attractive village there is surpassed only by Grosmont, five miles further on over Craig Syfyrddin, which has a remarkable church and the quietest of market squares in addition to its castle ruins. Although it serves as a local centre for shopping and social affairs, it has not been called upon to do much catering for visitors.

This route continues across the main road, the river and the railway just west of Llangua, and follows little-used rights of way to Llancillo and Walterstone Common. Thence it leads over to the lane leading down to the church at Clodock, the early religious centre for this Welsh territory of Ewyas. In later years, this became dominated by the Norman earthwork at Pont hendre – where the meadow path from Clodock joins the road which leads up to the stone castle of the de Lacies, in the odd rectangular earthwork at Longtown.

Like Grosmont, Longtown once had its markets and fairs, and it still has inns and shops. But for all their character and history, these places in the attractive broken country of woods and pastures, between the tourist-conscious Wye Valley and the Black Mountains, have been slow to see themselves as centres for visitors. Walkers may help to keep the surviving services in being, without disrupting their quietness.

3 BLACK MOUNTAINS AND ELFAEL HILLS

Pandy is an obvious access point on the Path. Nearby farmhouses, a guest house and three inns, one with a camping and caravan site, offer accommodation along the A465, which has a sparse bus service between Hereford and Abergavenny.

The main problem for the next stretch is the long Hatterrall Ridge, which rises ahead to 2,306 feet above sea level and provides a hard sixteen miles of walking to Hay-on-Wye. This is too far for anyone who is not in training; on the other hand, there is not much accommodation around the half-way mark, other than the Youth Hostel at Capel-y-ffin, and what there is tends to be booked up by pony-trekkers. There are old farmhouses on the Olchon side which have begun to cater for the quieter walking folk, and it is worthwhile trying to arrange for two more leisurely days, rather than one hard slog along the ridge.

The Path starts near the Lancaster Arms. Cross the field to a footbridge over the Honddu, and continue over the railway line past the conspicuous little castle mound. From here the route runs through Tre-fedw farm up to the crossroads at the col. The easiest way lies straight ahead, up the metalled track, but the Path descends steeply to the right, then climbs the end of the ridge leading to the Iron-Age hill fort of Pentwyn. This is the first conspicuous hill-top site along the route which stands any comparison with the great forts further north.

Signposts were parsimoniously provided in this National Park area, but the Path is clear along the ridge north of Pentwyn. The ways leading up from Llanthony and Longtown can be difficult to find among the fields and bracken of the lower slopes. The most direct route north from the fine ruins of the Augustinian Priory (tended by the Ministry of Works, but con-

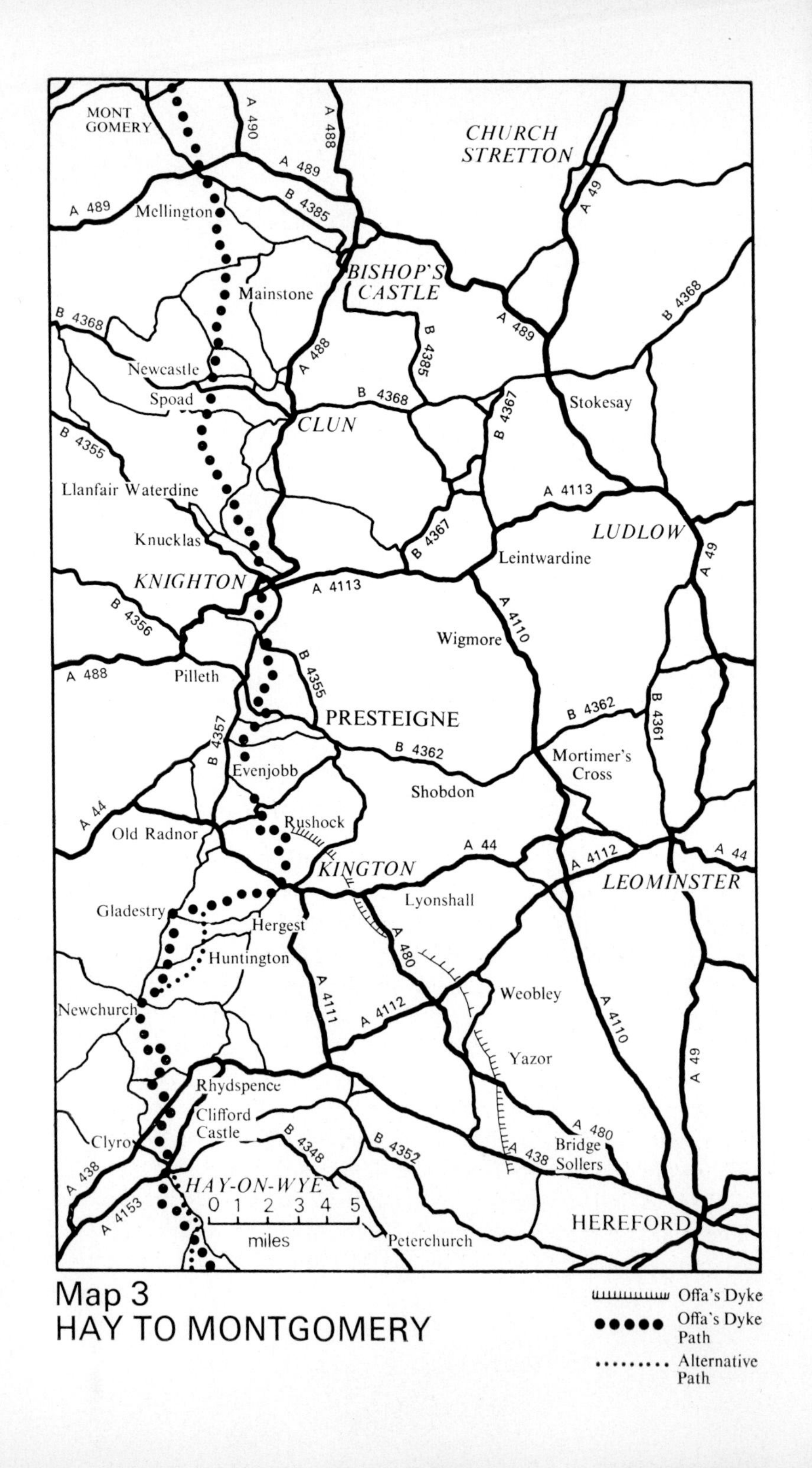

Map 3
HAY TO MONTGOMERY

taining an inn) leads up towards the site of the poet Landor's ill-fated mansion at Siarpal, then left to Loxidge and along the steep 'rhiw' path to the crest of the amphitheatre which cradles the Abbey ruins.

These 'rhiws' up the steep rock-strewn slopes must have been man-made, presumably for driving cattle and sheep up to the higher grazings in summer. Like the Dyke, they renew one's wonder at the muscle-power of our ancestors, for they can be found all along the Black Mountain 'daren' slopes.

On the other side of the ridge a field path runs north-west from the round tower-keep of Longtown Castle. It crosses a footbridge and follows the new road past Turnant Farm, turns left along the hill-foot track, and climbs the steep 'rhiw' up through the bracken towards the crest of the hill above the remarkable landslips on Black Daren. The three paths join on the featureless top at 1,983 feet.

From Black Daren it is possible to look back over the intricate land of villages and castles which lies between the barrier of the Wye gorge and the face of the Black Mountains, the even more effective natural barrier between England and Wales on which you now stand. There is only one record of a Welsh attack on the de Lacy castles which were built down there to dominate Ewyas, and from which William crossed into the deserted Honddu valley, soon after 1100, to found the hermitage which grew into the great Llanthony Priory.

Once on the top of Black Daren the Path breaks up into confusing sheep-paths, and the ridge from here to Pen-y-beacon is much more flat-topped than seems likely from the map. From the right there is a view back into Nant Honddu ('about an arrow-shot broad' – as Giraldus Cambrensis described it in his 12th century account of Llanthony); and from the left a patchwork of fields stretches out below into the Herefordshire plain.

It is surprisingly easy to lose one's bearings on this five-mile stretch. Waymarks have now been provided, but in bad weather it is better to take the paths and lanes from Llanthony, up the east side of the Honddu to Capel-y-ffin, then across and along the foot of the hill behind the Youth Hostel to join the road again where it comes out on the open mountain. The valley road carries a great deal of traffic in the summer, and any car travelling this route will need a driver who does not mind reversing and tight passing-places.

The Path, signposted only on Herefordshire stretches, avoids the last boggy stretch between the summit and Pen-y-beacon by turning eastwards to join the faint old track from the Olchon Valley. Along this comes the other alternative way from Longtown and Llanveynoe over the dramatic ridge of the Cat's Back. Instead of the gently angled descent along the track you can go on to enjoy the wide panorama from Pen-y-beacon, ('Hay Bluff' to Herefordians) and descend a hidden zig-zag 'rhiw' from the point, down to where *all* the alternative routes join on the mountain road below.

The Path, still unmarked in 1972, turns off to the left, following a less frequented surfaced lane past Maes-coch and Pen-yr-hen-allt Farms, and thence, via a battered burial cairn, along an overgrown route to Hay. Or you may walk further along the delightful turf, close-cropped by sheep and ponies to the remains of prehistoric burial mounds at Twyn-y-beddau. Here you turn off the mountain road along the ridge to Cadwgan farmstead, and down field paths alongside the boundary valley of the Dulas into the compact little border town.

If you have left a car behind at Monmouth or Pandy, you can take one of the infrequent buses back via Hereford. The next day you will then be able to visit the group of churches at Kilpeck and Abbeydore, Vowchurch and Peterchurch, up the Golden Valley, and the ruins of Snodhill Castle and Clifford Castle. But being car-borne again entails following the next stretch of Path, to Kington, by car. Those who want to walk on should find a bed for the night in Hay, and make an early start for Kington the next morning. You will find it hard to forego the exploration of all the shops and nooks and crannies of Hay – and the vast second-hand bookstore which spreads from the Castle through half a dozen other premises.

Leave Hay across the new Wye bridge, and follow the river north along the far bank. Pass the great Roman camp, of which little trace remains, and strike out along hedges and tracks to the A4153. The Path turns away westwards from the view to Clifford Castle, crosses to the other side of the wooded Bettws dingle beyond New Barn, and turns right to follow the metalled

Hay on Wye. A sign points the way, on the Radnorshire side of the river from the compact little fortress town

Rhydspence Inn. The fine half-timbered building, just on the English side of the border, was a halting-place on one of the old drovers' roads

Gladestry. A fairly typical small Radnorshire village on this stretch of the Path

lane for a mile. Approaching the head of the next dingle a track off to the right leads to little Bettws Clyro church, in a field with fine views across the Wye. Francis Kilvert took services there as curate of Clyro a century ago. Now his Diary has become famous as an evocation of this countryside and its people – though its warm references to young girls raise an occasional eyebrow! He took down from an old countryman the tradition of how Charles I's army marched along this route on August 6th, 1645 – 'riding two and two in the narrow lanes' – to the scanty accommodation at Old Radnor. This was immortalised in another Diary – 'where the King lay in a poor low Chamber and my Lord of Linsey and others by the kitching fire on hay; when the King was at his supper eating a pullet and a piece of cheese – the good wife, troubled with continual calling on her for victuals and having, it seems, but that one cheese, comes into the room where the King was and very soberly asked if the King had done with the cheese, for the Gentlemen without desired it.'

A path across the fields cuts the corner onto the lane from the fine old black-and-white Rhydspence Inn to Crowther's Pool. From this lane a grass track runs due north to a lane following the boundary between England and Wales. What is sometimes thought to be a Roman road runs west into Little Mountain and the strange little earthwork which looks out over Rhos-goch bog, where the black-headed gulls nest, and over to Painscastle. Henry III spent the summer of 1231 building there, but only green banks remain.

The Path follows the hedge to the right along open grassy top then turns sharply east, before Gilfach-yr-heol to join the lane to Newchurch. In the village, turn right off the Gladestry road in front of the cottages beyond the stream. Up the lane lines another pleasant stretch of hill-common on Disgwylfa. At the far end bear left past Hill House Farm, follow the road past Grove Farm, and take the track north to Stonehouse Farm. You cross the next valley at Gladestry (where there is an inn). The route swings back on the lane to the right before turning off between the cottages up to the green roads on Hergest Ridge. An alternative would be to continue eastwards from Disgwylfa along lanes and paths to Huntington. This is the quietest of the former centres of baronial power; the inn and post office are the only buildings on its little green. To the south, a lane goes through a farmyard to the isolated little church, and to the north another lane leads to the extensive earthworks and scattered stone fragments of the castle. On the Radnorshire side of the boundary stream a footpath runs down to a battered foot-bridge, across the Gladestry brook, and up through Upper Rabber to join the main route on the fine open grazing land of Hergest Ridge.

The Radnorshire stretches of the Path were among the first to be completed, with an impressive array of bilingual signposts, markers and stiles, in marked contrast with the blankness of Breconshire and distinct from more lightly-constructed English signs in Herefordshire. The differences tell you where you pass from Wales into England and help to identify the local highway authorities who can be commended, or condemned, for the condition of the Path. The Countryside Commission supervises and refunds the expenditure they incur.

This is the land of the white-faced Hereford cattle – more familiar to most as the great range herds of the American West, but this was the home of the breed before its character was fixed by eighteenth-century Herefordshire stockmen. Don't be too worried if you do find that one of the cattle in a field crossed by your path is a large wide-horned bull; there seems to be no record of a Hereford bull taking the trouble to charge after anyone without extreme provocation. You will find young bullocks and cows, which crowd round and follow you, much more unnerving although no danger unless you have a dog with you.

Walker's dogs are generally unwelcome, especially running loose before lambing time. Those who have allowed this have been partly responsible for the replacement of sheep by breeding herds and bulls, and the by-laws which have been brought in to allow them along the Path. Sheep pastures may provide better walking but cattle have a firmer place in Welsh border tradition.

The early Norman lords had great herds of cattle and Maud de Braos, when the family was in high favour with King John, presented the queen with – 'three hundred cows and one bull, all white with red ears', and boasted that she had over twelve thousand milking cows and so many cheeses – 'that if a hundred of the most vigorous men in England were besieged in her castle for a month and could only defend themselves by throwing cheese, let them throw as fast as they could, they would still have some left at the end of the month'.

Look to the north, over irregular hills of ancient rock, to the secluded Vale of Radnor, on its broad eastern side enclosed by hills along which you will again be following Offa's Dyke. Below, Old Radnor, with its beautiful church, offers better 'Crown' comforts than it offered to a crowned head in 1645.

The Path itself continues over the old racecourse, past the 'Whetstone' boulder and down into Kington. The church confronts you from a dominant position, but there is no trace of the castle which was nominally the head of a great barony. Centuries ago the town centre moved down on to the level ground, where you will find the narrow shopping streets jammed with traffic.

You can find accommodation in Kington, or if you have left a car back along the route, you can take a bus back along the A480 – the old Aberystwyth mail coach route. This follows the line of Offa's frontier for a while, crossing discontinuous (and not very recognisable) stretches of the earthwork at Lyonshall and Yazor. Among these orchards, black-and-white hamlets and fertile fields, the Dyke seems strangely unrelated to the great earthwork above the Tintern gorge. Sit back and let your eyes wander over some of the most unspoilt landscapes of rural England, back along the long western skyline and the great ridge of the Black Mountains. You will find yourself full of a sense of real achievement.

Mercian side and the line wavering across the hill as though its builders had to guess their line through thick woodland. The monument here commemorates a railway-promoting landowner and by the Presteigne road another 19th century stone was one of two, along the whole course, that identified the Dyke for passers-by. Descending to the road again there are fine views west to Radnor Forest and north across the Teme valley. Turning a short way on the Whitton road you find a stile in the angle of the lane leading off to the right at Rhos-y-meirch. A series of older Path stiles follow the line of the Dyke to where, after a ploughed-out stretch, it suddenly appears again on massive scale, commanding another 'traffic gap' above Jenkin Allis farm. On the crest the great earthwork dwindles abruptly to an ordinary-looking hedge-bank, leading past the golf-course, down into Ffrydd wood.

Below the wood you come to Knighton. Its original Mercian 'knights' may have been border rangers, and the Welsh knew their settlement as Tref y clawdd, '*The Town-on-the-Dyke*'. In 1970 a local Branch of the Offa's Dyke Association took this name and set about recovering an overgrown stretch of Dyke and riverside, which was threatened by factory extensions. In the face of official apathy and opposition they transformed it into a Park, where a stone monolith commemorates the official opening of the Path, and they have bought the old school, adjoining it, so that the Tourist Board and Countryside Commission can provide a Welsh Border Information Centre and Youth Hostel there. The town still has rail services to Shrewsbury and you can get back to a car left here.

From the Park, the Path along the riverside (also restored by the Tref y clawdd Society's initiative) crosses river, railway and road to climb Panpunton. From the moderate-sized Dyke on top you look down on the winding Teme and the railway sweeping up to the viaduct below Knucklas castle hill. You follow the Dyke to the triangulation station on Cwm-sanaham Hill, with another demarcation-point making a right-angle in the Dyke. From here you look down on a valley, full of legends of Arthur and Guinevere and Giants, of Dafydd Ddu and the Devil at Llanfairwaterdine. From that hill, beyond the mounds of Knucklas Castle, came a princely medieval sword and three

Offa's Dyke Stone. One of the two 19th century mark stones stands at the summit of the road to Presteigne. It gives the unlikely date of the first year of Offa's reign for the earthwork

The Path to Panpunton, restored by the Tref y Clawdd Society, with a foot-bridge provided by Shropshire County Council and the Countryside Commission

Offa's Dyke, ascending Llanfair Hill. From Selley Crag and Garbett Farm the massive tree-covered earthwork runs up towards the highest point on its course 'from sea to sea'

Clun Forest Shepherd. The Craig Farm shepherd has to keep a careful eye on flocks which graze these wide pastures, and which are at risk from strange dogs and careless visitors

The Dyke from Spoad Hill looking back to Llanfair Hill. A fine open stretch of the earthwork, seen in winter with Radnor Forest in the distance. No right-of-way has yet been granted, and the Path follows the lane on the right

Clun. The great Saxon church looks across to the high mound and keep of the de Say and Fitz Alan Lords who ruled this area. The Dyke crosses the hills in the background

Bronze Age gold necklets, when it was ploughed in 1954.

Follow a modest Dyke down at an angle by Brynorgan cottage and over awkward crossings of the little valleys to reach Garbett Hall and the track alongside the Dyke which turns through to the great bank mounting up through the trees onto Llanfair Hill.

Apart from a modern barn, by the Dyke, there is scarcely another building in sight on the rolling upland of Clun Forest. It remained wide open range land until a century ago when the fences were laid out, but they do not mask the full magnificence of Offa's Dyke as you follow it from crest to crest, then along the parallel lane to Springhill farm. This stands on the road which follows the line of the ancient ridgeway, along which flint implements from the England chalklands were traded in prehistoric times. They have a fine collection of flint arrowheads and other tools in the little museum in the old Town Hall in Clun. It also has a Youth Hostel and other accommodation, and a great Norman church and Castle ruins, in 'the quietest' – (according to A. E. Housman) – or was it 'the drunkenest'? – little town – 'under the sun'.

From Springhill the Dyke runs sharply down to one of the most interesting farmhouses on the Path, at Lower Spoad, with some remarkable timber work in the great cruck-built barn and a carved hunting scene of dogs and deer on the overmantle.

Somewhere in these parts the Saxon, Wild Edric, hunting in Clun Forest, seized his fairy wife – who, according to chroniclers, went with him when he made his peace with William the Conqueror in 1068 – a strange story of turbulent times; they say their wild hunt still rides these hills.

Across the river the Path now follows the Dyke from Bryndrinog northwards over Graig Hill, then left where the lanes join in the Mardu valley and right to pass Mount Cottage. Beyond this, striking up to the right, the Dyke runs, a great terrace on the slope, past the ruined Hergan Cottage and piped spring of clear, cold water, to the road. Here the team of diggers whose work we have been following seem to have missed the line and dug fifty yards too far. A weak bank, at an odd angle, joins their work to the stretch which Fox deduced to have been built by another gang.

From here Offa's Dyke follows a switchback course across

a series of small steep valleys, in the deepest of which stands Mainstone Church. To the north there were difficulties in obtaining the rights of way to where the Dyke reaches another 'control point' on the Kerry Hill ridgeway, and negotiations have been even more protracted on the Montgomeryshire side.

The tracks along the Dyke offer wide views over the Plain of Montgomery to Corndon, and north to Long Mountain and the Vale of Severn. They join in a deep surfaced lane through Cwm, and break into paths again past Mellington Hall (Country Club and caravan park). Emerging from the gatehouse on the long drive, the road winds past a high castle mound on the Dyke, to the Blue Bell Inn at Brompton crossroads.

From Lower Spoad, the seven miles of this sort of Dyke walking are enough for most of us in a day. If your driver has met you here you could go back to visit England's smallest borough at Bishop's Castle before you come to the still smaller and sleepier Welsh borough at Montgomery. You might stay at Mellington or the Blue Bell, or perhaps your feet might carry you the three and a half miles to Montgomery along the rather tangled lowland Dyke.

5 ACROSS THE VALE OF SEVERN

The Dyke cuts across the Plain of Montgomery with brutal military directness, but without the deliberate impressiveness of parts of the upland Dyke. It provides pleasant walking, in good weather, but suffers by comparison with the stretches you have crossed.

You realise at Brompton, why some car-borne travellers begin to doubt whether the Dyke exists: it formed too convenient a quarry in the days of turnpike roads. Turn off the Montgomery road into Brompton Farm drive, through the gate on your left, to the far corner of the field. Up through the bushes you will find yourself on top of the familiar bank. You stay on it, except to skirt Ditches Farm on the west, until the Dyke and present boundary coincide at the Lack Brook. Then you continue alternately in Wales and England and sometimes right on the administrative boundary, with a foot in each country, to the Chirbury road.

The 'Ditches' farm we passed is a reminder that the ancient name, all along the boundary, was Offa's *Ditch* – or *Offediche* as it was recorded here in the thirteenth century, when it marked the division between the 'Hundred of Chirbury' and the Marcher Lordship of Montgomery.

Chirbury, over to your right, was probably a stronghold fortified by Aethelflaeda, daughter of Alfred the Great, and later a small monastery and borough, but those with time for a historic detour will usually turn towards the ruins of Montgomery Castle, pitched on this high crag by Henry III in 1223 against the rising power of Llywelyn the Great. It would be easy enough to spend a day walking round the little town (less than a thousand people uphold the dignity of its Mayor and Corporation) and beyond the castle to the great Iron Age hill fort of Ffrydd Faldwyn and the 'Mound-and-bailey' earthwork of Hen Domen. This Nor-

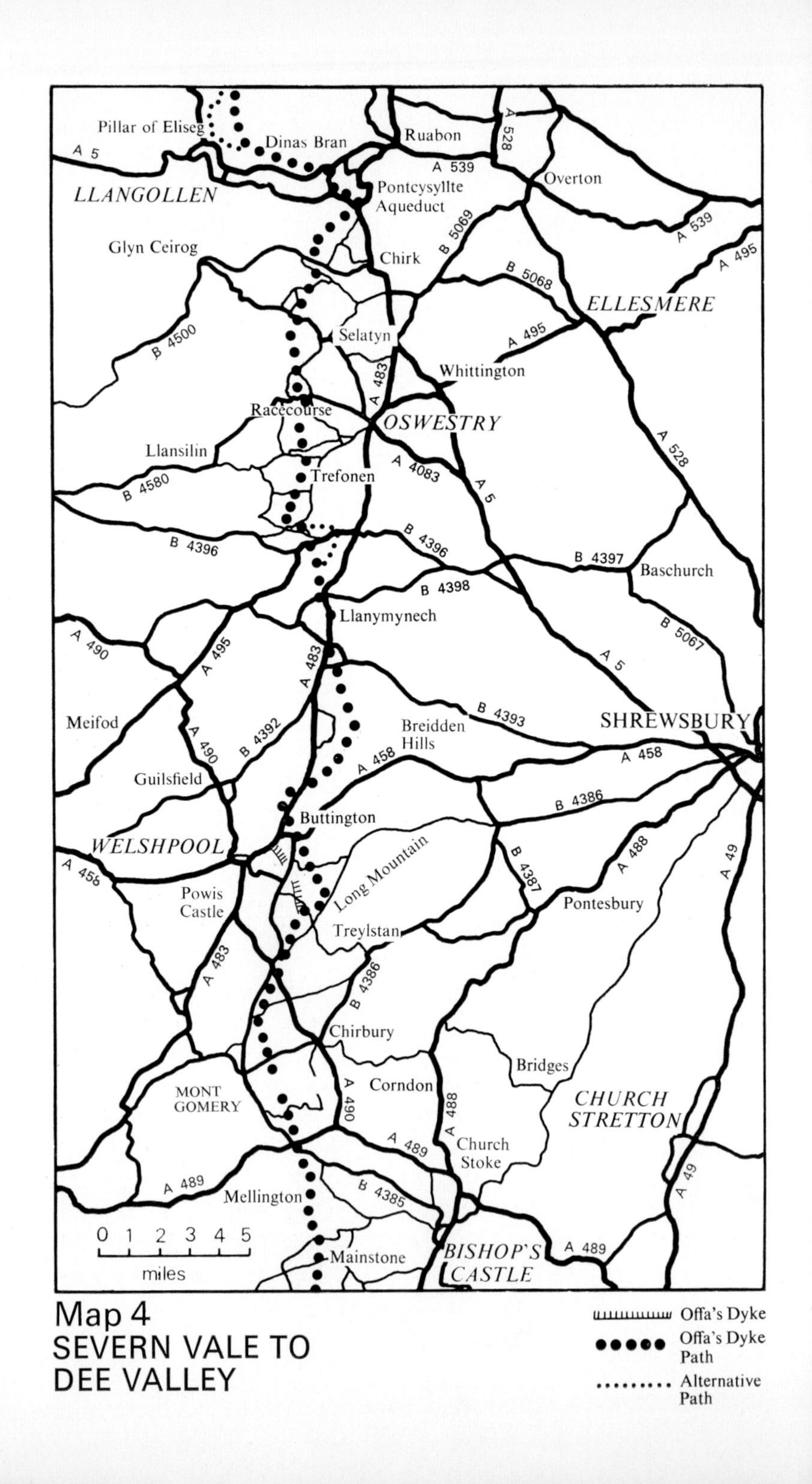

Map 4
SEVERN VALE TO
DEE VALLEY

man timber castle looked down on the site of the Roman Camp which guarded the ancient Severn ford of Rhyd whyman. Hen Domen has been meticulously excavated for several years as the site of the original Montgomery, founded by Roger, first Norman Earl of Shrewsbury, but it compares poorly with the massive Hall of the contemporary Earl of Hereford which you saw at Chepstow. An 'Old Montgomery' forming the southern end of the present town would explain the otherwise inept line of its Town Walls, which the Welsh were able to storm on at least three occasions. But some walkers may prefer the sort of guidance a friend claimed to have received here when he asked the way to the castle. He was surprised to be directed down the street since he was sure he ought to go up by the Town Hall. 'No' replied his informant, firmly, 'That's not the "Castle"! That's the Green Dragon.' But a former Mayor has nailed this libel. There is no 'Castle' in Montgomery apart from the historic one which is being extensively excavated and restored by the Ministry of the Environment.

The unswerving Dyke walker will cross the Chirbury road and follow tracks and paths alongside the Dyke, until it fades out approaching the marshy 'Devil's Hole', then turn across the meadows to Salt Bridge. Here another of those remarkably straight roads (not Roman, probably 18th century turnpikes), which point direct to Montgomery Castle, crosses the little Camlad; the only river which rises in England and flows into Wales.

The Path cuts back to the Dyke and follows it parallel to the Forden road, then along the road itself past the Nantcribba crag of a long-destroyed castle of the Corbets of Cause. From the A490, which joins it, the Path follows the Dyke again, behind the hamlet at the junction of the Welshpool and Leighton roads.

As you follow the steep Long Mountain road, you will wonder why Offa did not run the Dyke straight to the river, saving four miles of awkward digging, or else keep to a lower contour which would have given a reasonable line. Fox thought that the Princes of Powys (whose successors built the red castle crowning the ridge south of Welshpool, on the far side of the Severn) had established their claim to the Leighton meadows: a military critic saw it as a fall-back line for Mercians who might be driven back from the river by Welsh attacks; but as in other stretches Offa's dominant aim seems to have been to see and to be seen. If you climb out of the deep hollow on to the Dyke bank, your view ranges far back over the South Shropshire hills, up the Severn valley and over the rolling tiers of hills beyond.

The Royal Forestry Society restricts access to the great re-wood groves below the next stretch of the Path, which follows a track to an overgrown stretch of Dyke, then another track above 'Offa's Pool'. It crosses the road near Pant-y-bwch Farm and continues up to the top of Long Mountain. It is possible to follow the line of the Dyke more closely, to Pentre, especially if you are aiming for the choice of accommodation and facilities which the busy town of Welshpool offers.

The alternative way down to Pentre passes a strange building on Moel-y-Mab – the great compost tank from which all the meadows of Leighton were fertilised. This, together with the redwoods, the church and the high-towered mansion, were the estate improvements of a 19th-century Liverpool banker; a challenge, perhaps, to the Herbert lineage and Clive-of-India wealth at Powis Castle across the river – but the Earl of Powis, having come to an arrangement with the National Trust, still lives in his home, while there are no Naylor descendants at Leighton.

It is a pity that there seem to be no proposals to restore paths along the Dyke itself between Pentre and Buttington, though apart from another original traffic gap by the Hope lane, it has few well-preserved features. The Path follows a more strenuous route up the lane opposite Pant-y-bwch, then over field-side stiles up to the gentle summit, with wind-battered plantations. It goes on along the west rampart of Beacon Ring, which commands the great circuit of hills and valleys and the wide Shropshire plains to the north-east. In the evening you will feel the presence of ancient travellers along this way, from the legends of Arthur and his hosts, to Henry Tudor, on his way to Bosworth and the throne, and the shadowy Elystan, founder of the last "royal tribe" of Wales, killed here and buried at Trelystan. If you have a car, this little half-timbered church, completely isolated on the other side of Long Mountain, demands a pilgrimage.

The Path from Beacon Ring, through the plantation and down the spur to Stone House, aligns itself with the road and railway bridges across the river at Buttington. Here faint traces of the great Dyke, which you have followed continuously for these last few days, turn towards the river, not to be recognised until it starts out northwards, four and a half miles downstream.

Between Welshpool and Trewern you should find better accommodation than Rhonabwy, man-at-arms of Powys, found hereabouts in the 12th century, when he and his companion came to 'an old black hall, whence issued a great smoke – the floor full of puddles and mounds and slippery with the mire of cattle' and 'in the living part, an old hag making a fire with chaff and raising intolerable smoke, and offering for supper, "barley bread" and cheese, and milk and water'. For them there was no better bed than the couch made of 'a little coarse straw full of dust and lice, with the stems of boughs sticking through where the cattle had eaten the straw at the head and foot,' which Rhonabwy left for the yellow calf-skin on the floor.

It might be worth such lodgings though, to have a dream such as Rhonabwy dreamed – of all the men and panoply of King Arthur and his court, scattered across the plain of Severn and up the Long Mountain to Caer Digoll – the 'Beacon Ring' we crossed. His dream tested the memories of generations of the wandering bards of Wales, and the translation of it in 'The Mabinogion' may be a fitting prelude to your well-earned rest.

If you have ended a day at Buttington (where the Danish marauders were cut off by English and Welsh forces in 894 and reduced to eating their horses before the desperate remnant escaped to Essex), the next day's walk only used to be recommended as a way of completing that continuous line 'from sea to sea' without walking too much hard road. The flood-banks on the west side of the Severn are passable summer walking where they are grazed, rough otherwise, but never so bad as was the jungle-bordered bog which the Montgomeryshire Canal had become. Until this was cleared, in 1971, even the A483 offered better walking to the oasis at Pool Quay. The site of another great Cistercian Abbey at Strata Marcella, on this stretch, is almost as unrecognisable as Grace Dieu back near Monmouth.

To reach the Severn flood-banks, it is safer to pass the

signposted gate on the A483 to go through the next gate on the right beyond Pool Quay Church. From the flood-banks ramblers will look longingly at the steep Breiddens, and if you can add an extra day to your itinerary you would indeed find better walking there, up to the Hill-fort and the Pillar to Admiral Rodney – even more oddly land-locked than the Naval Temple above Monmouth.

Beyond Rhydescyn cottages the Path leads across the flood-control gates and back to Derwas bridge, over the 'New Cut'. A sign points across the flood-levelled fields to faint traces of Offa's Dyke, which need the eye of faith to follow them to the new footbridge over the Bele Brook. This leads to where the Dyke runs north disguised first as flood-bank, then as a lane and finally as a broad shapeless ridge in the fields to the B4393. Beyond this remains of more massive stretches continue to the site of the station at Four Crosses, and over the meadow beyond to the main road. The old Cambrian railway might have offered an alternative to the miserable mile of main road to the Vyrnwy bridge and Llanymynech, but the bridges were pulled out and the gaps wired before the idea had been considered. The still overgrown abandoned Canal, detouring west over its ponderous Vyrnwy Aqueduct, may some day be opened up as a more pleasant and peaceful, if longer, alternative. The terrain has its own interest for those who can read the scars of forgotten railways and mineral lines, leading to the jagged quarries in the hard limestone rock.

You can find accommodation at Four Crosses, or perhaps most amusingly at Llanymynech, where you might sleep on the very line of the Dyke, on the Shropshire side of the main street, where the front rooms are in Wales and the back rooms in England.

Montgomery. Looking from the churchyard, the town square of the smallest corporate borough in Britain drowses below the ruins of its royal border castle

Crossing the Chirbury road. The Dyke running north is reduced briefly to the size of an ordinary hedge bank – possibly by the activities of 18th century builders of the straight 'Turnpike' roads

Sign and Stile at the Camlad crossing. The recent work of the Countryside Commission and Montgomeryshire County Council, seen here at Salt Bridge, has marked out a more attractive route along the Dyke

Leighton Hall seen from the Dyke Path, looking across the Severn Valley to Powys Castle and the Berwyns in the far distance

Offa's Dyke at Carreg y big. A massive stretch from Baker's Hill, where the right-of-way has been disputed, continues beyond the road crossings, guarded by the old farmstead

6 THE DYKE AND THE DEE

The old advantage of the back rooms of Llanymynech, on the English side of the Dyke, as an oasis for thirsty Sunday travellers from a 'dry' Wales, will have no future significance. The Path continues in Montgomeryshire. It climbs from the deep lane to the Old Quarry, then west along the slope of Llanymynech Hill, one of the redeeming stretches of delightful walking in this Severn basin sector. There is an easier ascent from the end of the metalled lane to where the Path follows Offa's boundary, along the western rampart of a vast ancient hillfort which enclosed the plateau. The Romans had certainly mined rich ores of copper, lead and silver from the 'Ogof' Cavern. Unguarded shafts to their narrow galleries can be seen near its entrance, by the Golf Course. Later the Earls of Shrewsbury built a Castle of Carreghofa here, and up to 1213 it figured prominently in Welsh border warfare and in royal silver-mining projects. But it has disappeared so completely that no-one seems to know where it stood.

It is a pity to have to follow the Path down the steep face and across to Porth-y-waen, when you can continue along the top of Blodwel Rocks and follow the Dyke along the edge of Lynclys Hill. There are vast views across the Shropshire plain on one side, and the intricate valleys leading up into the Berwyns on the other. This path comes out by the lane almost opposite the 'Red Lion', on the A495. But you will have to follow hard roads back to the line of the Path beyond this. From Porth-y-waen the Path, west to Cefn Farm, winding through Nantmawr and over Moelydd Hill, avoids the direct road-slog to Trefonen, alongside the quarried and broken line of Offa's Dyke. Here the way becomes more pleasant, along lanes and paths. Approaching Pentre-shannel it climbs onto a short stretch of Dyke, which is the first full-scale and undamaged example we have encountered in the past fifteen miles.

The pig-farm which you pass through at Llanforda Mill is not one of the attractions of a pleasant valley, but you are soon across the stream into the cool rides of Llanforda Wood. You turn up the neglected paths, searching for the line of the Dyke and the quaint stone seat which was built on it when these rides were the pleasance of the demolished Hall. Eventually you have to give up the struggle to follow the Dyke and turn up to the more open summit of Oswestry Racecourse.

The seven or eight miles of Offa's Path from Llanymynech to the B4580 road may be enough for the day. It is pleasant to walk down into Oswestry and do some more exploration there.

Oswestry is the 'Marcher' centre for this stretch, and an appropriate 'baronial' base for a night or two. This was a strange place for St. Oswald, a Northumbrian king, to have been campaigning. Wat's Dyke, the earlier frontier mark of Mercia, runs through the eastern suburbs of the town towards the huge ramparts of Old Oswestry; one of the mightiest and most accessible of the great Iron-Age hillforts.

The Norman castle in the town was granted by Henry I to Alan, believed by Shropshire's greatest historian to have been the son of Fleance by a daughter of Gruffydd of Wales, to whose court Fleance had fled when Macbeth's assassins killed Banquo, his father. Fleance was killed or imprisoned by Gruffydd for this presumptuous romance, but his son, established at Oswestry, became the ancestor of two of the proudest families of Britain. William fitz Alan gained the other great Lordship whose gaunt castle ruins we saw at Clun, and his descendants went on to attain eminence as Earls of Arundel. His brother Walter returned to Scotland and became the ancestor of the royal house of Stuart. You would hardly suspect that the battered castle mound in the market place, where on the bustling market days you can still hear Welsh spoken by the country people, could have had such a vivid history or such importance as a border stronghold.

The last good walking stretch along the Dyke itself runs another eight miles from Oswestry's Old Racecourse to the Dee, but the Path and rights of way have still to be decided at the start, where from the crossroads you can see the Dyke

Dinas Bran. The Path passes the ruins, towering above Llangollen, of the castle of the Welsh princes of Northern Powys, whose ancestors here were the rivals of the Mercian kings

Monument by Selatyn road. The other 19th century marker, where the Dyke crosses from Selatyn Hill and dips steeply across the old turnpike road between Oswestry and Glyceiriog

Pontcysyllte Aqueduct. Leaving Offa's Dyke, which has gone on into the coalfield areas, the Path crosses the Dee by Telford's early 19th century, cast-iron aqueduct, one of Britain's major monuments of industrial archaeology ascending Baker's Hill on a massive scale from the Llanfyllin road. You may have to be content with the view from the road to Carreg-y-big. Beyond this farm you go along another fine stretch of Dyke, but the Path has been diverted to the east of the magnificent earthwork which runs from the isolated farm-house of Orseddwen to a salient on Selatyn Hill. This seems to have been one of Offa's sighting points and the main alignment swings back now across the lower slopes towards the mouth of the Vale of Llangollen. The Dyke pitches too steeply to be followed across the Selatyn road (where it is marked by an inscribed stone tower) down into the dingle. You follow the tracks on the east of it, above the quarry and down the lane across by Craignant farm, then along the Dyke again to cross another lane and across a very steep, wet and overgrown dingle to the next road. Another fine but overgrown stretch of Dyke leads to a green lane, beyond which you look across the Ceiriog Valley to see Chirk Castle, perched like a picture-book fortress on the hill beyond. Tradition paints a vivid picture of the ambush, in this valley, of Henry II's expedition which set out from Oswestry in 1164.

Chirk, like Powis Castle, is more of a stately home than a medieval castle now. It was a late baronial stronghold on lands taken from the Welsh princes of Northern Powys after the final conquest of Wales in 1282. It had to be largely rebuilt after the Civil Wars, when the Myddletons, who still live there, took Parliament's side. The paths up the Dyke and on the drive to the north-east entrance lodge, are only open in the summer months (when the Castle is also open to visitors).

Angling up left, by Crogen Wladys, the Path crosses the ridge to follow lanes and roads to the west of the surviving stretches of Dyke. It seems a pity not to be able to follow the last good stretch that comes to Telford's Holyhead Road at Plas Offa. Beyond that, along a last fragment of Dyke, then the A483 Canal bridge across to the north side to follow the towing path along another of Telford's great civil engineering projects to one of his masterpieces of industrial archaeology, the Pont-Cysyllte Aqueduct. For the first time in the world metal was used here on a major scale to make an aqueduct; a cast-iron trough over a thousand feet long and a hundred and twenty feet above the turbulent Dee. It was opened in 1805 and still carries pleasure boats, though the height upsets some walkers, who prefer to admire the aqueduct from the narrow stone bridge on the B5434, which is the official line of the Path.

Buses into Llangollen are more frequent on the north side of the valley, or you may find accommodation nearer the Path, for there is little of border history to be seen in Llangollen itself. The Vale has been used to catering for tourists for more than a century and there are better facilities than anywhere since the lower Wye valley.

From the towpath west of the B5434, a path to the main Llangollen to Ruabon road and a minor road to the right lead you to the drive of ruined Trevor Hall. Here you turn up at an angle through the plantations up to the open metalled 'Precipice Walk' – a fine bit of scenic engineering which is a sad reminder how little has been done in this country in this century to make it possible for people to admire beautiful scenery such as this, compared even with what was being done before that in the 18th and 19th centuries.

The Path keeps along this road, below the towering limestone scarp of Creigiau Eglwyseg, beyond the junction with the road which comes up from Llangollen and over into the upper valley of the Eglwyseg. There is little catering for travellers along the next seven miles of the official route, and there are some trackless stretches of moor to cross. It would be best to tackle this by an early start from Llangollen. This gives the chance to climb the last three hundred feet to the top of the isolated hill on which the princes of Northern Powys built their 13th-century stone castle within the earthworks of Dinas Bran, the legendary stronghold of their ancestors who fought against Offa and the Mercian kings. No town could grow around a site like this. The markets were held down by the church of St. Collen in the valley, seven hundred feet below and a mile away. Descending the west slope, paths and lanes will bring you to Valle Crucis, the fine Cistercian Abbey which these princes founded and endowed – a daughter house of Strata Marcella, whose blank site by the Severn we passed on that dull stretch by Pool Quay. These are considered the most attractive and interesting monastic ruins in North Wales. Beyond them, up on the right of the road, stands the Pillar of Eliseg. This is the remains of an inscribed stone Cross mounted on a tumulus, which is one of the most important surviving monuments for those Dark Ages, after the collapse of the Roman Empire, in which the frontier marked by Offa's Dyke came into existence. The almost illegible inscription lists the ancestors of the princes of Powys, back from Cyngen, who died at Rome in A.D. 854 and his great-grandfather Eliseg whose successes against Offa, or his immediate predecessor, it celebrated, right back to Vortigern and his wife, the daughter of Magnus Maximus. Magnus was killed in 383, while attempting to make himself Emperor of Rome at the head of the forces from Britain. The princes of Powys claimed a continuity which was almost unique in Europe, but a generation later, when the Welsh had accepted Bede's story that Vortigern brought the Saxons into Britain, the princes of Powys dropped him from their pedigree.

It is possible to cross the river by a footbridge a little way back towards the Abbey, and take paths and tracks past Abbey Cottage and Hendre to reach the narrow road from Llangollen to Minera; then to turn up through the gate facing Plas-yn-Eglwyseg bridge, up the valley and across to the cottage at Glyn and on past the ruined cottage beyond, to the ruins of Cae'r-hafod. The open mountain track with spectacular views down to Pentre-dwfr finishes at the odd outpost of Rhyl sea-front which provides welcome refreshments at the top of the well-known Horseshoe Pass. On a 'baronial expedition' you will be driven back to Llangollen with a good start established for the next day which crosses the long chain of Clwydian Hills now visible running northwards to the sea. A 'frontier patrol' may manage the two or three miles to accommodation at Llandegla, or the occasional buses from there along the main road to Ruthin.

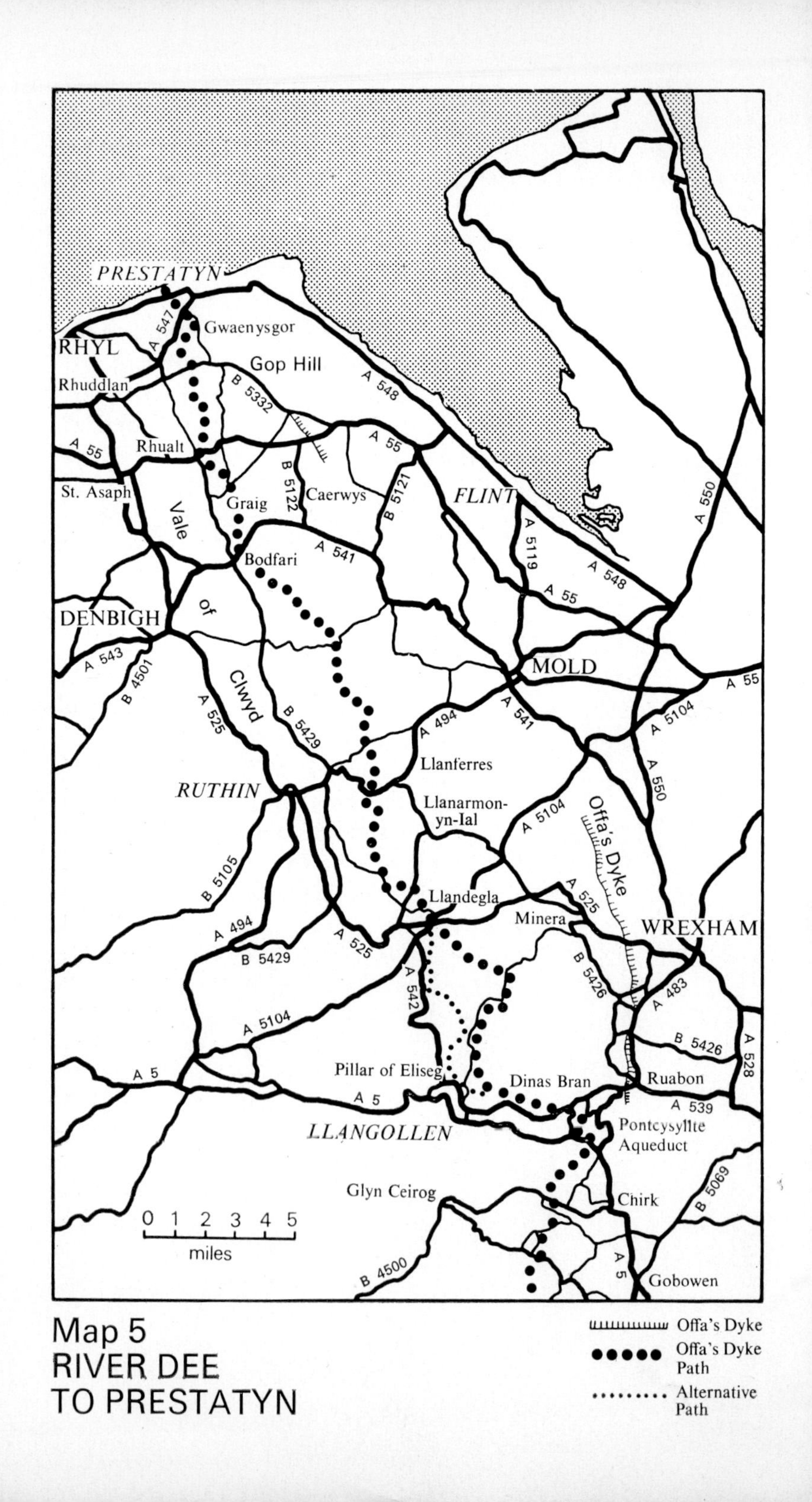

Map 5
RIVER DEE
TO PRESTATYN

7 CLWYDIAN WAY TO THE SEA

The last stretch of the Path offers walking most like that on The Pennine Way. The Dyke has been left behind, and you will only rejoin its line for the final mile to the sea. Instead the Path runs as far as possible across open hills; but you cannot escape from history in the Welsh Marches, and you will find yourself on the ramparts of great Iron-Age hillforts – like coiled stretches of Offa's Dyke – looking down on intricate patterns of farms, hamlets and fortress-towns.

There is a practical advantage in that this is the only stretch where a single One-Inch sheet, number 108 (Denbigh), is satisfactory and where you can follow the best stretches of walking from it. The end-to-end walker used to have difficulty even with 2½ inch maps on the designated route between where we left it on the 'Precipice Walk' and the start of the open hill footpaths on the Clwydians, ten miles further on, but Denbighshire, from a slow start, have made great improvements to the Path.

Starting from the narrow road, signposted to Minera and 'World's End', at the point where it turns down into the Eglwyseg valley, the Path continues at a higher level below the gleaming white crags of Eglwyseg Mountain, ascends an old drove track under Craig Arthur, and makes a difficult descent opposite the singularly isolated half-timbered manor house of Plas uchaf. It emerges from the plantation at the ford of the valley of World's End, with its abandoned mining tunnels. It is easier to continue along the top of the escarpment to join the 'Nature Trail', which continues round the head of the plantations to meet the Path route on the road where it climbs on to the open moor. It is difficult to identify the spot where the old track turns across the head of the stream and over the moor to Hafod Bilston. Some waymarking has been done, but map-and-compass work may be needed in mist or rain, and this is the only part of Offa's Path where gamekeepers have been encountered, maintaining a vigil against unauthorised disturbers of the grouse. It is only by Llyn Gweryd at the other end of this stretch, that fences and notices to keep out trespassers are obtrusively in evidence. Offa's Path has been remarkably free from these jarring reminders.

The Path over to Llandegla cannot be recommended, even for moorland-lovers, until the way from Hafod Bilston to Llandegla has been more clearly defined, either along the road, or the path to Trefyddbychain, if the obstruction of the direct path cannot be overcome. The alternative route from Plas-yn-Eglwyseg, by the Horseshoe Pass to Pentre-bwlch and field paths to the junction of the A5014 and A525 at Llandegla, provides a practicable alternative for walkers with maps who do not need waymarks and signs.

Beyond Llandegla church the field paths have been marked out across the Alyn. The only recognisable features of historic interest are the small caves in the low limestone ridge in the field opposite the old quarry lay-by on the B5431 at Perthichwareu. A complicated group of prehistoric burials were found when they were excavated a century ago. The Path crosses the road and goes westwards, along tracks and paths through Chweleriog. It continues up to join the lane, which has come more directly from Llandegla, at Tyddyntlodion, and continues along the hard road until you leave it and bear up along the edge of the plantation on to Moel y Gelli. Beyond it the sharper ascent on to Moel y Plas is the beginning of a fine stretch of open hill walking, through the grass and bracken, up to where gorse and heather spread a blaze of colour in the summer.

Beyond the surfaced lane from Llanarmon-yn-Ial (a pleasant little village with a fine large church and a little castle-mound), the Path follows a low line above the enclosed ground round to where a grey boulder, the Garreg Lwyd, marks an old way between Moel Llanfair and Moel Gyw down to Llanarmon. The Path continues at the same level, descending a spur to the farm lane which comes out just below Clwyd Gate on the main road between Mold and Ruthin.

If you walked all the way from Llangollen, twelve solid

Llandegla. Beyond the moors of Cyrn y Brain the Path leads on to fine open walking along the line of the Clwydian Hills

Llanarmon yr Ial. The attractive church in the pleasant valley lies to the east of the Path

Moel Famau from Foel Fenlli. From the entrance to the great Iron Age hillfort the view stretches north beyond the restored tower on the 1,820 feet summit

At Bodfari. The sign points south across the footbridge on the Denbighshire side. To the north the high Flintshire stiles mark the way to Prestatyn

Rhuddlan. Edward I's castle dominates the river channel which was cut by his workmen, on one of the most significant sites in Welsh border history

Prestatyn. The Path and Offa's frontier line come together again on the old cliffs looking down over Prestatyn, completing the way 'from sea to sea as Offa struck it out'

miles by the shortest route, this will be a good place to take a bus down towards Ruthin, or Mold, for a good night's rest and an early start tomorrow for the best day's hill walking along the whole of the Path. If you have your own transport, and have cut out some of the more tedious stretches, it will be worth the effort to end the day on a high note. Your driver goes on to Bwlch Pen-Barrass (the second turn beyond Llanferres for larger vehicles) while you walk over the summit of the A494, up the drive on the left and the track above Moel-eithinen Farm, with views to the east. To regain the views of the wide landscape over the patchwork of the Vale and the fortress site of Ruthin to the distant mountains of Snowdonia, you turn west to the col and face the great bulk of Foel Fenlli. Following the fence to the right, then angling back brings you up a track leading through the great ramparts of the most impressive of the hill-forts of the Clwydians. The ramparts, in some places larger than any section of Offa's Dyke, enclose a settlement area of more than twenty acres around the 1676 feet summit.

Old legends have it that Benlli, a Dark-Age tyrant who re-occupied the fort, was destroyed here by fire called down from heaven by St. Germanus when Benlli executed a Christian convert who arrived late for his work from the plain below; but no one has been able to show convincingly that these ancient forts were ever occupied again after Roman times.

Still, as you pick your way down the steep slopes up which generations of men must have toiled from their fields to their bleak homes your imagination can run over the dangers which must have driven them there. Your car down on the ample parking space and your 'baronial' accommodation in Mold, Ruthin or Denbigh will be all the more appreciated.

From Bwlch Pen-Barras a broad path angles off the main track and continues steadily upwards to the ruined tower on Moel Famau which commemorated the Jubilee of poor mad George III, tidied up by volunteers in European Conservation Year, 1970. This is the summit of the range, a modest eighteen hundred feet above sea level, but it commands far wider views than can be offered by many higher mountains, whose surrounding hills can never be so varied in their human interest as these views.

A less emphatic path down and along the crest of the range leads to the sharp descent to the road in the next pass, facing an even steeper slope up to the small but powerfully defended hill-fort on Moel Arthur (now a 'country park' area). The Path continues to the road at the head of the next pass. Tracks above the edge of the forestry plantation lead you out to the massive ramparts of Penycloddiau, ringing an area of more than fifty acres. Following the rampart along the west side of the fort, rather than the path across the centre, is like walking the Dyke again for more than half a mile.

Beyond the track at the head of the next pass, which was once reckoned the main road from Holywell to St. Davids, the Path turns off the ridge which would lead to the final summit Moel-y-parc, with its television mast. Trackways lead you down below Fronhaul, and field paths take you over to the lane behind Grove Hall, and on towards the elegant tower of Bodfari church, crossing tall, stepped Flintshire stiles to the A541.

You should go on to Denbigh, by bus or car along the main road from Bodfari, even if you are not intending to stay the night there, to walk round the spectacular town walls and the gaunt ruins of the Castle. After the shock of its capture in the Welsh rising of 1295 the Earl of Lincoln made the town defences incredibly strong, but after a generation or two of peaceful conditions the burgesses moved down from the cramped hilltop to live around their undefended market place – and to be burnt out again on at least two occasions, by Owain Glyndwr and by Jasper Tudor.

Mold, twelve miles in the other direction, has only the great mound of its castle, but it has the advantage of better links with the southern Clwydians and provides an opportunity for a car tour along the line of Offa's Dyke through the coalfield area. This will be a hard bit of rally training for your navigator as you search out the surviving stretches – from the A483 just north of Ruabon the Dyke stretches alongside the minor road running south-west, and continues in the fields beyond the B5097 to the Llangollen road; then back north (on the Chester One-Inch sheet 109) to the stretches crossing the minor road at Cadwgan Hall and by Plas Power Park, west of Bersham – among miners houses along 'Heol Offa' through Coedpoeth – over the scarred hill at Brymbo – down and along the Cegidog valley from the Roman site at Ffrith to the spur where the B5102 mounts on top of the massive bank of the Dyke, before the earthwork ends abruptly, half a mile short of the A5104. No one has found any trace of the Dyke for the next twelve miles through Mold to the faint earthwork which can be seen on the Old Holywell Racecourse and along the B5332 towards Gop Hill.

The Path that leads you on from Bodfari can only aspire to be a pleasant means of completing your way to the sea along the minor outposts of the Clwydians. These can still, from time to time, provide that breadth of view over populated plains to distant horizons which so often recurs along Offa's Path. The view extends over a whole range of humanity, from the great modern installations over on Dee-side to the little farms of the Vale of Clwyd and the rash of caravans and bungalows along the coast, but you are strangely detached from it all.

The Path itself follows steep lanes, narrow roads and footpaths up by a small hillfort on Moel y Gaer and along over Cefn Du before descending the west slope of Moel Maenefa to Rhuallt on the A55. An earlier descent to Graig, on the B5429 would give an opportunity to see the strange cult-figure at St. Beuno's Well, and the most important of the prehistoric cave-dwellings of the area on Ffynnon Beuno Farm. From here it is possible to make your way over paths and along quiet lanes towards Gop Hill; its hump, with the odd pimple of its huge burial cairn rising prominently over the rolling plateau to the north-east. On its lower slopes, north of the road, the last dimly recognisable stretches of Offa's Dyke can be seen.

The Path, opposed by forestry interests, has to climb back to follow the lane from Bodlonfa over Mynnydd y Cwm, before crossing the fields to Marian Ffrith, with its view to Gop on one side, to Rhuddlan on the other. The Dyke ends on Gop Hill in a form which suggests that it was never completed; one tradition has it that Offa died at Rhuddlan in 795 and that three years later the king of the North Welsh was killed in a great battle there. Perhaps the marking-out trenches for Offa's Dyke were left unfinished when the directing hand was withdrawn. But tradition has it that the line was marked out to the sea, and the sea is not far away now. You swing away from the desolation which the quarries have made on the once proud, hill-fort crowned Moel Hiraddug, away from the site of Dyserth Castle, that Henry III built and Llywelyn the Last demolished; and you pass the municipal desecration of the deep spring of Ffynon Asaph before you cross the Dyserth road, turn left on the next lane, then across more fields towards Tan-yr-allt. You might be excused for turning down to follow the foot of the old cliffs, but the Path, whose white waymarks are liable to be confused with yellow paint-splashes of a 'Nature Trial', leads back up along a cleared way through the brambles and gorse to the crest of 'King Charles' Bowling Green' and the view down to Prestatyn. Further along you join the road from Gwaenysgor and Gop descending in abrupt zig-zags to the long sweeping line of the Ffordd-las, 'the green road', carving its way through the straggling resort which has grown up at Prestatyn, to the coast of the Irish Sea.

It might have been better if the Path had kept a little further to the east and ended out on those empty dunes beyond the Golf links, but as you stride through the puzzled holiday-makers down to the shore and turn back into the sea-front cafe, it seems appropriate enough; more than a hundred and sixty miles of Path and more than twelve hundred years of history end here, in the present day, in the shape of a pleasant enough, unassuming holiday resort. But for many, looking back to the gorse-covered cliffs, there will remain a longing for the quiet hills, and the great boundary mark of the forgotten kingdom, and the Path which follows it back to Severn shore.

8 IN CONCLUSION

If you are aiming to walk the whole of the Offa's Dyke National Footpath and you are an average sort of walker, you will be well advised to allow three weeks for it. This applies whether you are doing a 'royal' or a 'Marcher' tour, with transport to and from the route, or an end-to-end walk, carrying all you need and finding accommodation where you can. If all goes well you should have two or three days to spare for looking round some of the more interesting places along the route – or just resting. If you plan to do it all in a fortnight it may prove a salutary form of penance, but leave little scope for pleasure. Even a practised walker may end the route with only memories of interminable hedges, stiles, fences, ups and downs, and only vague impressions of interesting places glanced at in passing, with no time to do more than study the map and follow the path to the next stopping place.

It is possible to cut down the 'car-and-foot' walk to a fortnight by leaving out the less interesting stretches of path, for example between Monmouth and the Black Mountains, between Hay and Kington, between Buttington and Trefonen, between Eglwyseg and Clwydd Gate and between Bodfari and Prestatyn. By doing that, however, you make it difficult ever to achieve the ultimate satisfaction of walking Offa's Path 'from sea to sea'. If you have only two weeks to spare it is better to aim to walk two-thirds of the way, and leave the other stretch for another time.

On the other hand there is perhaps more to be said for planning a week's route survey, if you are new to walking and to the Marches. There is no reason to fear that you will exhaust the interest of the route by a car-and-foot exploration of its most accessible stretches; you are more likely to whet your appetite for longer stretches of walking and a better understanding of the border features. Among those who consult this guide there may well be some who wish to see only the main features of interest along the frontier in one or two days, but they can select from the guidance intended for those who will spend the full three weeks along the route, perhaps in weekly instalments at yearly intervals.

We have followed the Path from south to north. It was the easiest way when there were no waymarks and detailed maps were needed – and it is still worth emphasising that however well you may be able to follow the One-Inch Ordnance Survey series while walking the open hills, country lanes and waymarked Path, you will need the much more detailed $2\frac{1}{2}$ inch maps on approaches to the more intricate field stretches of Offa's Path. It is important that you should not find yourself on the wrong side of a hedge which has been grown to restrain the wandering tendencies of Welsh Mountain sheep. Unfortunately the hedge and fence lines still shown on these maps are those which were mapped in the 1880's. Not all of them exist today, and there will be fewer still in years to come; but by then we may have newly surveyed maps and waymarked 'link' paths to follow. The Offa's Dyke Association is trying to produce strip maps for the Path, and guide leaflets to link routes, which will meet walkers' needs reasonably cheaply. You will find details in Appendix 8.

The south-to-north arrangement will be less convenient for those with keen archaeological interests, because Sir Cyril Fox's great survey follows Offa's Dyke in the opposite direction. Perhaps it will provide a way of distinguishing the keen students of archaeology from those whose interest is more general, but even the keenest student would be grateful for a more portable digest of the weighty volume in which Fox described the features of the great earthwork, and discussed its historical significance. To examine his evidence they may need to follow his direction, but a different angle of approach will not make Fox's main conclusions less interesting, or restrict your right to develop your own opinions. The Dyke is a feature which can only be properly appreciated by those who have followed it on foot, and realised what it must have involved in terms of planning, organisation and man-power.

If you wish to make a careful study of the Dyke and the other earthworks along the route, the spring is the time of year for your expedition, when the dead bracken has been levelled by the winter snows and before the leaves on bushes and hedgerows come out to mask the plan and the contours. Certainly the early months of the year are best for the southern stretch, not only for archaeologists, but for any walker, when primroses and bluebells are flowering in the Tintern woods and along the lanes, and before the leaves hide the dramatic views down into the valley below. April and May can be the best of months for Offa's Path, but they can be almost the worst for snow and wet and cold. These will bring more hardship to the new lambs and the sheep farmers along the route than to you, if you have taken good advice on footwear and clothing.

The Welsh Marches are to some extent sheltered by the higher mountain ranges to the west and have less rain than most of the hills of comparable height in other parts of Britain, though the day-to-day weather is equally uncertain. You need to be adequately shod and carry waterproofs which will not be too easily snagged and torn on the hedges and fences. If you do have to press on in hopelessly wet weather you will probably find it better to leave the line of the path and follow some of the more sheltered lanes which run parallel to it. Provided you can keep moving, it is no real hardship to get wet in the summer time – I have known walking parties who suddenly realised that they were enjoying it, and went on 'singing in the rain' – but you do need to be staying in accommodation where provision is made for wet and muddy clothing to be handled and dried. Country inns, with a tradition of catering for fishermen and huntsmen, tend to be more amenable than establishments which have only been used to the main streams of car-borne tourists, but hospitable farmhouses are best of all.

There are better chances of reasonable weather here than in most parts of western Britain, but if you are unfortunate, it may console you to read of the Kings who were driven back by the weather from their Welsh expeditions. Henry II, campaigning from Oswestry in 1165, crossed the Dyke to pitch his tents on the Berwyns, only to be driven back by 'a mighty tempest of wind and bad weather and rains, and lack of food' – and in rage had the eyes of his Welsh hostages gouged out. Henry IV, advancing against Owain Glyndwr in 1402, beyond Knighton, 'pitched his tents in a very pleasant meadow where everything seemed to betoken a calm and comfortable night, but in the first watch there came a flood of rain followed by a whirlwind which overthrew the King's own tent, where he might have been killed if he had not been sleeping in his armour!' He returned 'bootless and weather-beaten back'.

Every season of the year has something different to offer along this route, and for those who live within fairly easy driving range, there may be a good deal to be said for walking Offa's Path in week-end instalments through the winter, spring and autumn months, and keeping yourself in condition for more strenuous exertions on paths such as the Pennine Way in the summer. There are only a few parts of Offa's Dyke Path which ought to be avoided in mist: the Black Mountains provide the only stretch where a compass may be essential for keeping proper direction, rather than as a means of checking that you are reading your map properly, and even there interesting lower routes can be followed as alternatives.

One of the things you will probably notice is that once you are away from the Lower Wye and North Wales stretches where tourists are numerous, the people of the Border will almost always wish you a good day when you pass. Often they will be prepared to join in a longer conversation and show an interest which may seem flattering, but is a combination of border courtesy and border caution, and you must not presume too much on it. You have to live a long time in these parts before you are really accepted, though there are far more comings and goings than in many parts of rural Britain.

Although a good deal of the Path lies in Wales, you will not pass through many places where Welsh is in general use, though there are some signs of revival. For any traveller who is content with the English assumption that the name of a place is just a convenient label, there is only the occasional difficulty of an apparently unpronounceable name. But for those who like to join in the old game of 'guessing the meaning', the list in Appendix 5 may give the place-names along the Dyke a real fascination.

APPENDICES

1 Navigation

The essential map for planning a general approach to Offa's Dyke Path is the Ordnance Survey Quarter Inch special sheet, 'Wales and the Marches'. This covers the whole route, showing the main roads, towns and villages, hills and valleys, in a clear attractive form.

The O.S. 1 inch maps, unfortunately, are very awkwardly divided in relation to the Path. Only No. 108 (Denbigh) gives a full stretch of the Path and adequate cover of the roads on either side. For the rest, it is all edges and corners, and you will need all of the following: No. 117 (Bala and Welshpool), No. 118 (Shrewsbury), No. 128 (Montgomery), No. 129 (Ludlow), No. 141 (Brecon), No. 142 (Hereford) and No. 155 (Bristol and Newport).

Since 1971 signposts, waymarks and the tramping-out of a recognisable line over ground cleared of undergrowth by the local highway authorities, have made it possible to follow almost the entire length of Offa's Dyke Path from these 1 inch maps, aided by simple route descriptions given in this book, or in the leaflet which has been published by the Ramblers Association. For any variations from the route you will need the more detailed guidance which only the O.S. 2½ inch maps can provide. These are immeasurably more interesting and informative, but for an end-to-end walk – where up to 25 sheets are needed – they are an expensive proposition. The most useful sheets are ST 59 (Chepstow) SO 51, 41, 31 and 32 (Monmouth to Pandy), SO 23, 24 and 25 (Black Mountains to Kington, replacing 1 inch sheet 141), SJ 15 (Llandegla to Foel Fenlli) and SJ 07 (Bodfari-Dyserth). New editions of O.S. maps may mark the Path distinctively, but not older sheets.

To meet the difficulty and expense of using existing O.S. maps, a series of strip maps is being prepared, to be completed on nine or ten double-sided A.4 sheets, based on black-and-white or 2 colour reproductions from O.S. 2 inch outline sheets. Details may be obtained by sending a stamped addressed envelope to The Offa's Dyke Association (address, Appendix 8).

2 Clothing

Any reasonable outdoor clothing will do for short trips along Offa's Dyke Path in the summer months, but whole-day walks or more extensive expeditions along the route will call for clothing in which you can go on through rain without too much discomfort. A good rambling (or golfing) jacket, capable of resisting a shower, will need to be supplemented with a lightweight anorak or over-jacket in proofed nylon, and perhaps overtrousers as well.

Provided you keep warm, the main consideration is that things carried in pockets and rucksacks should be kept dry (putting them in plastic bags will help to make sure of this). Clothing liable to get wet should be of a kind which can be wrung out and dried easily, without suffering too much in appearance and shape as a result.

An ordinary cord or tough cloth cap which can be rolled up and carried in a pocket will keep the rain out of your eyes, the anorak hood away from your face, and serve as a useful hand-hold over barbed wire. Only on the hills, and other stretches in Spring, is bare-legged walking really practicable. For the rest you need trousers which give adequate protection against brambles, nettles and thorns. Jeans and wool-and-nylon oversocks will stand up to this as well as climbing trousers and long stockings, especially if the socks are protected by anklets, which also help to keep stones and grit out of your boots.

Far more difficult paths than any to be met along this route have been walked by people wearing tennis shoes, but a stout pair of walking boots will give greater protection, and save detours around cattle-trampled gateways and muddy stretches of lane. Do not go in for rock-climbing boots which are made flat, stiff and short in the toe and are entirely unsuitable for walking. 'Sprung sole' walking boots, with 'Commando' or 'Vibram' soles, are the best. Break them in well, and treat the uppers with dubbin or neatsfoot oil so that they can be flexed like a glove and do not rub your ankles or catch on your heel. Unless you are trying to imitate the self-scourging medieval hermits (like William de Lacy of

Llanthony who wore his armour until it rusted away), don't try to walk any distance in Wellingtons or long boots.

3 Equipment

Some walkers feel that they are not getting the right kind of exercise unless they are carrying a large, cumbersome rucksack, but most people will get more pleasure if they are burdened with as little as possible. However, you need to be able to get all the things you require into one convenient holder, and a rucksack with a lightweight frame, will be a worthwhile investment for border patrols. A simple change of clothing with extra pullover, socks, moccasins or sandals, toilet kit, a small first-aid wallet, a torch and matches in a waterproof container, and a plastic water-bottle (or a vacuum flask if you must have a hot drink), will meet your basic needs.

A good quality lightweight, down-filled sleeping bag will be necessary if you have not booked accommodation and wish to take advantage of any kind of shake-down which can be offered. With a waterproof cover, you can sleep out in it at a pinch, but for any assured enjoyment from sleeping out you need specialist advice on lightweight tents and camping equipment, and to be willing to carry at least another ten pounds weight above the fourteen or so which is the maximum sensible load.

A useful catalogue, covering the whole range of items you may need to buy for a Dyke Path expedition, is issued by Y.H.A. Sales, 29 John Adam Street (price 5p).

4 Accommodation

There is a wide range of accommodation in the area, including three-star hotels in Llangollen and the other main 'resort' centres, two- and one-star accommodation in other market towns, and country house hotels scattered along the route. Walking away from the car will involve using less luxurious, but perhaps more interesting alternatives, in inns, bed-and-breakfast houses, farmhouses – and farm buildings, and Youth Hostels.

HOTELS AND INNS. A few hotels along the route concern themselves mainly with catering for seasonal holiday-makers, but most are at least equally involved in the social and commercial life of the market towns in which they are situated, and you will find a good cross-section of the life in their bars and public rooms. Bed-and-breakfast prices are generally well below 'resort' or city levels for comparable accommodation. A number of Inns in the market towns and in the smaller villages offer accommodation at substantially lower rates, with similar opportunities for meeting local people.

'GUEST' AND 'BED-AND-BREAKFAST' HOUSES. There are guest houses in the same price range as the less expensive hotels which cater more exclusively for holiday visitors – some in an excellent and friendly way. Some are geared to serve walkers and fishermen; other rather unimaginatively cater only for car-drivers arriving late and departing early on their way to the coast. There are 'bed-and-breakfast' houses which extend the price range downwards to very inexpensive levels. Some mainly provide accommodation for people working locally; in others a housewife is using a spare room to give her an extra interest and a little 'pin money'. It is almost impossible to know what standards to expect; they are only vaguely related to the price. An enquiry at the nearest shop or pub does not always produce a reliable assessment – you will seldom get a really positive comment, good or bad, from the people you meet along the Welsh border.

FARMS. Most of these, at present fall into the 'pin money' group and you are more likely to be welcomed as a new face than as part of a commercial venture. Some now provide camping and caravanning sites or let empty cottages, and this gives an opportunity of establishing family 'base camps' from which the more energetic members can set out on walking expeditions of two or three days along the Dyke Path.

YOUTH HOSTELS. There are some lengthy gaps between the seven hostels which stand reasonably near the line of the Path, and the three or four which stand some way from it. They are only open to members of the Y.H.A. (address, Appendix 8), who can obtain meals, at some, and simple accommodation at low prices.

CAMPING AND CARAVANNING. There are only a few places along the route, as yet, which offer facilities for base camps or for caravans, but a number of farms will allow casual camping at the usual rates. Planned sites with toilet facilities will probably develop with Camping Club encouragement (Appendix 8).

ACCOMMODATION LISTS. The Offa's Dyke Association have

issued a list of places along the route, and the proposed Centre at Knighton may be able to provide more comprehensive grading and booking facilities in co-operation with the Tourist Boards.

5 Welsh Place Names and Pronunciation

On the main roads leading across the border, you will see the *Croeso i Gymru* notices giving you a *Welcome to Wales.* They also introduce you to one of the complications in the game of 'guessing the meaning'; the way in which the usual *c* of *Cymru* (Wales) has been changed to *g*. In the same way, after certain words, *m* changes to *f*, so *Mynwy* (Monnow) gives you *Sir Fynwy* (the shire of Monmouth), and *Maesyfed* (Radnor) gives you *Sir Faesyfed; b* also changes to *f*, so you get *Sir Frycheiniog* (Breconshire); *d* changes to *dd* as in *Sir Ddinbych* for Denbighshire; and *t* changes to *d* so that *Trefaldwyn* (Montgomery) becomes Sir Drefaldwyn. Similarly *p* is liable to change to *b* (as in *Sir Benfro* – Pembrokeshire) and *ll* to l; the initial *g* before *l* or *w* is liable to be dropped – so that *Gwent* (East Monmouthshire) appears behind its ancient fortress as *Caerwent*, but in the modern Welsh for Chepstow as *Casgwent*.

The Welsh have their own way of pronouncing the alphabet; the use of *w* as a vowel, the equivalent of the English *oo*, and the more frequent use of *y*, with the sound of *u* in *cut*, or if *i* in *pin*, causes much of the first bewilderment. You will get by if you remember that *dd* is English *th* (*mynydd* – mountain – is pronounced 'mun-ith'); that *c, g,* and *s* are always hard (k, gu, and ss); that *ch* is breathed on, as in *loch*, that single *f* is English *v*, and *ff* gives the softer *f*; that *r* is always trilled; and that for *ll* you should 'put your tongue behind your top teeth and hiss like a gander' – but if you make a noise somewhere between *l* and *th* it will be sympathetically received. *A, e, i,* and *o* are long (*a* as in *father, e* as 'a' in *gate, i* as 'ee' in *feet*, and *o* as in *note*) when they carry a circumflex or come before *b, ch, d, f, ff, g, s,* or *th* as single consonants; otherwise they are short as in English. *U* has a short *ee* sound.

There is a great difference between the English and the Welsh attitude to the names of places. Most English place names were originally simple descriptions, but where the language changed, the names remained, as convenient labels, so that even in areas where no Welsh has been spoken for hundreds of years, people keep on making a rough shot at the old Welsh farm and field names. The Welsh, on the other hand, have seldom been content with a simple description – they have had to make a song about the place, and as their language has changed, they have brought their place names up to date in meaning and in spelling. The odd result is that while Welsh place names are interesting for this national guessing game, it is only the limited number of names recorded in early manuscripts which can be used in the way that English place names are used, to help the study of early history. Along the border it is strange to find that the oldest names, even in some places on the Welsh side of the Dyke, are old English, such as *Radnor* (*red bank*) and sometimes oddly disguised, like *Prestatyn,* really *priest's ton,* another Preston!

The middle stretch of the Path, in particular, is a land of 'hopes' – an old Mercian word for a valley. It has been mutilated into *ock* in Rushock, and *ob* and *jobb* in Cascob and Evenjobb. *Bage* or *batch* generally means a steeper valley. *Bury* or *burf* a fortified place; *yatt* or *gett* a gate; *ley* a clearing; and *hay* a hedged enclosure, are also common. To complicate things further there are some good Norman-French names such as Montgomery, and the less obvious Hatterall (*haterel* – 'crown of the head') and Mold (*Mont haut,* or Latin – *Monte alto* – 'high mount'), and Kymin, Clyro, Pilleth, Clun, Spoad and such, where experts hesitate even to suggest a meaning.

COMMON WORDS IN WELSH PLACE NAMES

Welsh plurals are usually formed by adding – *au.*

A aber *river junction, or mouth*
adwy *gap, passage-way*
afon *river*
allt *steep slope*

B (for mutations see under P : e.g. *bandy – pandy*)
bach *little*
bedd *grave*
betws *small church*
blaen *head, source*
bran (brain) *crow* (*crows*)
bron *breast, slope*
bryn *hill, mound*
bwlch *pass*
bychan (fechan) *small*

C cae *field*
caer *fortress*
cam *crooked*
carn *cairn, rocky hill*
carreg *stone, rock*
castell *castle*
cefn *ridge*
celli *grove, copse*
clawdd *dyke, hedge-bank*
coch *red*

coed *wood*
collen *hazel*
cors *bog*
crib *crest (jagged)*
craig *rock, crag*
croes (crog) *cross, cross-roads*
crug *knoll, tump*
cwar (el) *quarry*
cwm *valley*

D (for mutations see under *T: e.g. dafarn – tafarn*)
dan *below, under*
deri (derw) *oaks*
din (as) *fortified hill*
disgwylfa *look-out, viewpoint*
dol *meadow*
du (ddu) *black*
dwfr *water*
dyffryn *vale, valley*

E eithin *furze, gorse*
eglwys *church*

Ff (for *F* mutations see *B* or *M:* e.g. *fach–bach, fawr–mawr*)
ffin *boundary*
fford *way, road*
ffos *ditch*
ffynon *spring, well*
ffridd *wood, sheepwalk*

G (for mutations see under *C:* e.g. *gam – cam*)
glas, gleision *green, blue*
gwaun *moor, upland grazings*
gwern *alder swamp*
gwyn (wen) *white, fair*
gwynt *wind*

H hafod *summer dwelling*
hen *old*
hendre *winter dwelling*
heol *road*
hir *long*

I isaf *lower*

L (for mutations see under G eg *las – glas*)
llan *enclosure, church*
llidiart *gate*
llwyd *grey, brown*
llwyn *grove, bush*
llyn *lake*
llys *hall, mansion*

M march (meirch) *horse*
maen (meini) *stone (s)*
maes *field, plain*
maer *steward, bailiff*
mawr *big, great*
melin *mill*
melyn *yellow*
moch *swine*
moel *bare hill*
mynydd *mountain, moorland*
mynach *monk*

N nant *brook, dingle*
neuadd *hall*
newydd *new*

O ogof *cave*
onnen *ash tree*

P pandy *fulling mill*
pant *hollow*
pen *head, top*
pentre *village*
pistyll *spring, spout*
pont *bridge*
pwll *pool*

R rhiw *slope, slant track*
rhos *moorland*
rhyd *ford, across*

S sarn *causeway, old road*
sych *dry*

T tafarn *inn*
tarren *cliff, rock outcrop*
tri (tair) *three*
troed *foot*

tir *land, territory*	ty (tai) *house*
tomen *mound*	tyddyn *small holding*
tre (f) *hamlet, settlement*	

U uchaf *upper, highest*

W (for mutations see under Gw : e.g. *waun – gwaun*)

Y y, yr, 'r *the*	ystrad *vale*
ynys *island*	ysgubor *barn*

6 The Law and the Traveller

by Quentin Edwards, Barrister-at-Law

Offa's Dyke Path is made up of various kinds of highway as the maps and text in this book show. Roads need no explanation for we all know them. Bridlepaths may be used by both pedestrians and riders of horses, ponies, donkeys (or mules!) and bicycles. Footpaths may be used by pedestrians only and no wheeled vehicle may be taken on them, except prams and cycles.

In law Offa's Dyke Path is being completed as a continuous public right of way. That description is a complete statement of the user's rights : h has no more and no less. The route is *public*, so any citizen may use it without asking the leave of the owners of the land over which it runs, but his *right* to the route is a right to use it as a *way* only, in other words simply for the purpose of passing along it.

Much of the route runs along open moorland and hilltops. Some of it skirts a National Park and some of it runs over common land. Nevertheless every foot of its surface belongs to an owner; the roads to local authorities and the paths and bridle roads mostly to private individuals. The only limitation upon their rights as owners is the right of the public to pass along the road or path.

No one walking or riding along the route should forget the owner's position. The name 'National Park' sometimes misleads people into thinking that they are entitled to wander in a National Park as they can in the parks in their home towns. This is not so; the ownership of land in National Parks is precisely the same as elsewhere.

Some of the route runs through or skirts by common land. Contrary to popular belief the public have no right to roam at will across rural commons. The land is so called because various land-owners in the vicinity have rights in common over it – such as the right to graze their sheep on it. Commons should therefore be treated as private property.

The wild open look of the countryside through which the route runs may also mislead some into thinking that the land is no one's property. On the contrary, the farmers along the Welsh border make their living from the land just as much as farmers everywhere else, though they may graze the land rather than cultivate it intensively.

All this means that the public who use the route may not roam about as they please in the fields and moors through which it passes. If they do so they are trespassers and liable to be treated as such. Furthermore they are almost certain to do more damage than they realise. Sheep and cattle may be frightened and driven from their proper grazing ground. Although the farmer probably has his working dogs, your dogs will be unfamiliar to the animals so keep them under proper control. Townspeople often do not appreciate that if animals are chased or made to run about they may lose weight (and so value) and, if pregnant, may abort (at great loss to the farmer).

Summer fields of grass may be a valuable growing crop of hay; grazing trampled and fouled is an asset spoiled; every square yard of a cultivated field is in actual use; farm buildings, though they may be deserted when you see them, are part of the farmer's capital.

Never forget that the land and animals are the farmer's raw material; they are his living and if abused he suffers just as the business man if his factory is broken into or the salesman if his car is put out of action.

As the public are entitled to use the paths to pass along they may legitimately take a reasonable rest when exercising that right. Clearly a walker is entitled to sit by the path and enjoy the view or eat a meal. But camping on the route, except at the places set aside for that purpose, is not lawful. Nor is the lighting of fires or any destruction of the surface of the ground – as by digging a hole for litter. Take the litter with you – after all, you brought it – and put it in the bins which you will find from time to time. If everyone puts a greasy bundle under a stone or in a bush the route will be a loathsome place in a few years.

Some people love to pick flowers, but even on routes as long as Offa's Dyke Path this temptation ought to be resisted: if you pick them the rest of us cannot enjoy them. As for the blackberries in the wayside hedges and the cranberries by the path, passers-by have picked them since time immemorial and custom is part of the common law; so pick them in season if you like but be careful not to damage or make openings in the hedges or to stray on to private land.

A great judge has rightly described the law of highways – which is only another name for public rights of way – as the law of give and take. So when you use the Path take only your rights and give the respect fairly due to the rights of your neighbours over whose land you pass.

7 The Country Code

When following a National Footpath, take care to avoid damaging farm property by remembering this Code:

Guard against all risks of fire

A cigarette thrown away or a pipe carelessly knocked out can start a raging inferno. Take care with camp or picnic fires and ensure that they are properly put out.

Fasten all gates

Animals, if they stray, can do great damage to crops and to themselves too. Even if you find a gate left open, always shut and fasten it after you.

Keep dogs under proper control

Animals are easily frightened – the chasing of a ewe or cow may mean the loss of valuable young.

Keep to the paths across farmland

Crops are damaged by trampling at any stage of growth. Remember that grass grown for hay is also a valuable crop.

Avoid damaging fences, hedges and walls

If you force your way through a fence or hedge, you will weaken it. If stones from walls are rolled down slopes they may injure people, animals or farm property.

Leave no litter

All litter is unsightly. Broken glass and tins and plastic bags are dangerous; they very easily harm livestock. So take your picnic remains and other litter home with you.

Safeguard water supplies

Water is precious in the country. Never wash dishes or bathe in somebody's water supply or foul it in any other way.

Protect wild life, wild plants and trees

Wild flowers give more pleasure to more people if left to grow. Plants should never be uprooted. Trees are valuable as well as beautiful and should be left alone.

Go carefully on country roads
Country roads have special dangers. Blind corners, hump-backed bridges, slow-moving farm machinery, and led or driven animals are all hazards for the motorist.
Respect the life of the countryside
The life of the country centres on its work. The countryman has to leave his belongings in the open; roads and paths run through his place of business, and the public are on trust. Be considerate.

8 Useful Addresses

Automobile Association, Fanum House, Leicester Square, London W.C.2 H7 LY.
British Tourist Authority, 64 St. James's Street, London S.W.1.
The Camping Club of Great Britain and Ireland Ltd., 11 Grosvenor Place, London S.W.1.
Caravan Club Ltd., 65 South Molton Street, London, WIY 2AB
The Council for British Archaeology, 8 St. Andrew's Place, Regent's Park, London N.W.1.
The Countryside Commission, 1 Cambridge Gate, Regent's Park, London N.W.1.
The Offa's Dyke Association, Knighton, Radnorshire LD7 1AA
The Ramblers' Association, 1 Crawford Mews, London WIH 1PT
Royal Automobile Club, 85 Pall Mall, London S.W.1.
H.M.S.O. (Stationery Office), P.O. Box 569, London S.E.1.
Wales Tourist Board, Welcome House, Llandaff, Cardiff CF5 2YZ
Youth Hostels Association, Trevelyan House, 8 St. Stephen's Hill, S. Albans, Hertfordshire.
Y.H.A. Services Ltd., 29 John Adam Street, London W.C.2.

9 Helpful Publications

And Far Away by Garry Hogg. The only account of a walk along Offa's Dyke (before the National Footpath was designated). Published 1946. J. M. Dent & Sons, Ltd.
An historical Atlas of Wales by W. Rees. A summary of Welsh history, locating the main events and features. Published 1951. Faber and Faber.

Bed and Breakfast Guide. The Ramblers' Association.

Brecon Beacons, National Park Guide. Published 1967. H.M.S.O.

British Camping Sites. Haymarket Press Ltd., Gillow House, 5 Winsley Street, London, W.1.

Caravan & Camping Sites & Farmhouse Accommodation in Britain. British Tourist Authority.

Dean Forest and Wye Valley, National Forest Park Guide. Published 1956. H.M.S.O.

District Guides are published by most of the District Councils along the route.

Offa's Dyke by Sir Cyril Fox. A detailed archaeological description of the earthwork, with some chapters discussing its historical significance. Published 1955. Oxford University Press.

The Offa's Dyke Path. ed. A. T. Roberts, Ramblers' Association leaflet.

Public Rights of Way and Access to the Countryside by Quentin Edwards and Peter Dow. Price 35s. Published 1951. Shaw and Sons Ltd., 7 Fetter Lane, London, E.C.4.

Regional Guide to Ancient Monuments – No. 3. Midlands; No. 4. South Wales; No. 5. North Wales. H.M.S.O. An archaeological introduction, and a brief account of each of the monuments under the guardianship of the Ministry of the Environment. Separate guides and leaflets are published for the main sites.

Rural Landscapes of the Welsh Borderland by Dorothy M. Sylvester, Macmillan, 1969. 548pp. A detailed historical geography.

The Shell Guide to Wales by Wynford Vaughan Thomas and Alun Llewelyn. Published 1969. Michael Joseph Ltd. and George Rainbird Ltd.

Welsh Border Country. The long-established book of this title by P. Thoresby Jones, published in 1938, is now replaced in Batsfords series by a guide written by Maxwell Fraser, an even more knowledgeable author.

The Welsh Marches by Millward and Robinson (In Landscapes of Britain series), Macmillan Educational, 1971.

Wales Tourist Board Guides: North Wales, Mid-Wales and *South Wales*. Booklets giving up-to-date information. Also free leaflets and accommodation lists.

Index